UNIVERSITY OF NORTH CAROLINA
STUDIES IN THE ROMANCE LANGUAGES AND LITERATURES
Number 87

THE MARGUERITE POETRY
OF GUILLAUME DE MACHAUT

THE MARGUERITE
POETRY OF GUILLAUME
DE MACHAUT

BY

JAMES I. WIMSATT

CHAPEL HILL

THE UNIVERSITY OF NORTH CAROLINA PRESS

DEPÓSITO LEGAL: V. 631 - 1970

ARTES GRÁFICAS SOLER, S. A. - JÁVEA, 30 - VALENCIA (8) - 1970

TABLE OF CONTENTS

	Pages
INTRODUCTION	9
CHAPTER	
I. THE "DIT DE LA FLEUR DE LIS ET DE LA MARGUERITE"	13
II. THE INFLUENCE OF "LIS ET MARGUERITE"	30
III. PIERRE OF CYPRUS AND THE IDENTITY OF MARGUERITE	40
IV. THE TRANSCENDENT MARGUERITE	60
INDEX	67

INTRODUCTION

Marguerite is one of the famous names of fourteenth-century love poetry. The poetic lady of this name is, like her eminent Italian counterparts Beatrice and Laura, a person of ultimate charm, beauty, and mystery. Unlike the ladies of Dante and Petrarch, however, Marguerite was celebrated by not one but several writers, notably the Frenchmen Guillaume de Machaut, Jean Froissart, and Eustache Deschamps. Their Marguerite poems in turn exercised an important influence on Chaucer's Prologue to the *Legend of Good Women* and are related to Thomas Usk's *Testament of Love* and perhaps to another Middle English work, *Pearl*.

As with so many women of literature, one of the most interesting questions about Marguerite is her historical identity. The name was very popular during the Middle Ages, so that while the poets might all have been writing about one particular lady, they might as probably have had several ladies in mind. Or Marguerite could have been simply an ideal in the minds of the writers, for the French poets all identify her with the flower signified by the name —the daisy— and the word in addition means *pearl*. Taking into account such symbolic implications, we can surely imagine that the poets were celebrating an exemplar which had no existence outside of their minds. This question of identity has importance not only for understanding the historical situations of these poems, but also for comprehending the nature of medieval symbolism.

The general development of Marguerite poetry, its origin and growth, is also a matter of substantial significance since the Marguerite poems are among the more lively and valuable literary

10   THE MARGUERITE POETRY OF GUILLAUME DE MACHAUT

products of fourteenth-century France. The relative importance of Machaut and Froissart in this development has an appreciable bearing on an assessment of each poet's achievement. And the evolution of the Marguerite poems is significant to the Chaucer scholar for its relevance to the English writer's daisy imagery, his fictive devotion to the flower, and the daisy-like figure of Alceste.

This monograph provides substantial new material on the Marguerite poems which throws considerable light on these problems. Perhaps most importantly, it supplies an edition of the previously unedited *Dit de la fleur de lis et de la Marguerite* of Machaut, which rivals Froissart's *Dittié de la flour de la Margherite* as the best of the longer French poems in the group and is a work which Chaucer evidently read and used. Of comparable importance for the study of these works are the historical identifications made here. An acrostic in Machaut's Sixth Complaint, previously unnoticed, reveals that work as probably the original Marguerite poem and evidences a nearly certain connection of Machaut's poetic lady with Pierre of Cyprus. Having thus made an identification of the lover, we are better assured of the lady's historicity, and we have an example rare in medieval literature of the poetic first person being known to represent a patron of the writer. Furthermore, a correlation of Pierre's activities with those of the poet allows us to make probable suggestions as to the identity of Marguerite and the occasion of each of Machaut's three Marguerite poems.

Among other things, this study indicates that Machaut is the originator of most of the Marguerite imagery and of the narrative motifs used by his successors in these poems; and it strongly suggests that the daisies of all of the poets, including Chaucer, had real-life counterparts, but at the same time embodied ideals of womanhood.

The first two chapters contain an edition of the *Dit de la fleur de lis et de la Marguerite* and a discussion of the poem's relationships with other French poems and with Chaucer's works, notably the Prologue to the *Legend* and the beginning of the *House of Fame*. The historical circumstances of Machaut's poems are the subject of Chapter III: I point out the acrostic which shows that the Sixth Complaint was written for Pierre de Lusignan to his

Marguerite, and I use this historical clue and others in the poems to fix the place of the works in Pierre's career and the life of lady, who was probably Marguerite of Flanders. In the final chapter I discuss the possible significance of the name to Pierre and to the poets who celebrated it; the contents of the poems and historical clues both suggest that the name symbolized something beyond its temporal referents.

Chapter I

THE *DIT DE LA FLEUR DE LIS ET DE LA MARGUERITE*

The importance of Guillaume de Machaut's contribution to the vogue of Marguerite poetry has seemed limited, since the *Dit de la Marguerite* has up to now been his single known and printed work among the Marguerite poems, while both Froissart and Deschamps produced several such works. As a matter of fact, Machaut's role is much greater than has appeared, for two more of his works should be classified as Marguerite poems: the *Dit de la fleur de lis et de la Marguerite*, ignored by editors and by others confused with the *Dit de la Marguerite*, has not been hitherto published; and an acrostic which allies the Sixth Complaint to the group has remained unnoticed.

It is surprising that an important work of the famous Machaut has remained unedited for so long, especially when its title proclaims probable relevance to Chaucer's *Legend*. However, V. F. Chichmaref evidently considered the *Dit de la fleur de lis et de la Marguerite* not properly part of his collection of Machaut's lyrics;[1] and, perhaps because his efforts were disrupted by World War I, Ernest Hoepffner did not include it in his publication of the longer poems.[2] Indeed, three other significant poems of Machaut found themselves in the same editorial limbo between the edition of the lyrics and that of the longer *dits;* but they have been

---

[1] *Poésies lyriques de Guillaume de Machaut,* ed. V.-F. Chichmaref, 2 vols. (Paris, 1909).
[2] *Œuvres de Guillaume de Machaut,* ed. Ernest Hoepffner, Société des anciens textes français, 3 vols. (Paris, 1908-21).

published elsewhere. The *Dit de la Marguerite* and the *Dit de la Rose* were included by Tarbé in his early anthology of Machaut's work,[3] and Karl Young edited the *Dit de la Harpe*.[4] Though Professor Young in publishing the *Harpe* expressed an intention to edit the *Dit de la fleur de lis et de la Marguerite*[5] (henceforward *Lis et Marguerite*), he seems never to have found time to do it. Others may have been misled as to the actual existence of the poem by John L. Lowes' confounding of *Lis et Marguerite* with the *Dit de la Marguerite* in his encyclopedic article on Chaucer's Prologue and the Marguerite poetry.[6] Lowes quotes Tyrwhitt's speculations made in the eighteenth century about possible influence of *Lis et Marguerite* on Chaucer, but Lowes then seems to assume that *Dit de la Marguerite* is the poem to which Tyrwhitt had referred, though the two works are clearly different.[7] Another factor which may have contributed to the neglect of this poem is that *Lis et Marguerite* is extant in only one manuscript, while all other works of Machaut can be found in at least three and generally in six or more.[8]

Fortunately for the purposes of an edition, the unique copy is found in a very good manuscript, Bibliothèque Nationale fonds français 22546 (fol. 71v-73v). According to Hoepffner this manuscript belongs to one of the two best collections of Machaut's work —the most complete, with the best readings, and apparently written in the lifetime of the poet, who "doubtless watched over their execution."[9] The manuscript copy of *Lis et Marguerite* bears

---

[3] *Œuvres de Guillaume de Machaut*, ed. Prosper Tarbé (Paris, 1849), pp. 65-67, 123-129.

[4] "The *Dit de la Harpe* of Guillaume de Machaut," ed. Karl Young, in *Essays in Honor of A. Feuillerat*, ed. Henri M. Peyre (New Haven, 1943), pp. 1-20.

[5] P. 16n.

[6] John L. Lowes, "The Prologue to the *Legend of Good Women* as Related to the French *Marguerite* Poems and the *Filostrato*," PMLA, XIX (1904), 593-683.

[7] Pp. 593-595.

[8] See the tables of contents of the Machaut manuscript collections provided by Chichmaref, I, lxxvi-lxxvii, and by Friedrich Ludwig, ed., *Guillaume de Machaut: Musikalische Werke*, (Leipzig, 1928), II, 43°.

[9] *Œuvres*, I, xlvi, li. B. N. français 22546, along with 22545, forms one collection. The other collection to which Hoepffner refers is B. N. français 1584.

out Hoepffner's evaluation. In the 416 lines of the poem there are few apparent scribal errors. The poem that the manuscript presents is a technically finished work, one of the better examples of fourteenth-century French poetry.

The fact that *Lis et Marguerite* is found in but one manuscript points to composition late in Machaut's writing career (d. 1377). If, as I suggest, it was written for Philippe le Hardi, Duke of Burgundy, and Marguerite of Flanders, their year of marriage —1369— seems likely. I will discuss this possibility in Chapter III.

Each of the thirteen divisions in the following text is headed by a large capital in the manuscript.

Ci commence le dit de la fleur de lis et de la Marguerite [10]

    Qui saroit parler proprement
    Des couleurs et le jugement
    Faire des fleurs et des flourettes,
    Pour quoy les unes sont blanchettes,
    L'autre est jaune, l'autre est percette,   5
    L'autre ynde, l'autre vermillette,
    N'i a celle qui n'ait verdour
    En esté et diverse odour,
    Ou qui n'ait ou greinne ou semence,
    Ce seroit moult belle science;   10
    Mais je ne congnois creature
    Qui tant des secrez de nature
    Sache, qui me sceust aprendre
    Pour quoy c'est ne la cause rendre,
    Comment que c'est chose certeinne   15
    Que pluseurs s'en sont mis en peinne
    Et fait tout leur pooir sans feindre,
    Mais onques ne poient ateindre
    Ad ce que la chose sceue
    Fust clerement et congneue,   20

---

[10] I am indebted to Professor James Atkinson of the Department of Romance Languages of the University of North Carolina at Greensboro, and to Professor Rupert Pickens of the Department of Romance Languages at Chapel Hill for their assistance on several readings in the preparation of this edition.

Fors tant que Nature le vuet,
Qui de son droit faire le puet;

Et comment que moult petit vaille
Tel scens com Nature me baille,
Vueil emploier a deviser, 25
Au mieus que je y saray viser,
Les vertus de la fleur de lis,
Qui mout est pleinne de delis,
Et aussi d'une fleur petite
Que l'en appelle marguerite, 30
Ou il n'a point de mesprison,
Si vueil faire comparison
De lors bontez, de lor affaire,
Au mieus que je le saray faire.
Or me doint dieus commancement 35
Bon, et milleur definement,
Et moienner par tel maniere
Que ceste ouevre a ma dame chiere
Plaise. Car s'elle li agrée,
De moy en sera mieus amée, 40
Et aussi ceuls qui la liront
Pour s'onneur mieus l'en ameront.

Il est certein que jhesucris,
Si com je truis en mes escris,
Dit dou lis en ses chansonnettes 45
Paroles courtoises et nettes,
Et vesci les propres paroles
Qui je ne tien pas a frivoles,
Car il y a moult grant substance
Et mout bele signefiance: 50
"Com le lis entre les espines
Est m'amis entre les meschines,"
Et c'est a dire entre les filles
Qui tant sont sages et soutilles
Qu'en cest valée de plour 55
Gardent leur corps de deshonnour

Et de pechie qui tue l'ame
Quant femme chiet a cause en blame.

Or regardons que c'est a dire,
Car mout est noble la matyre   60
Dou lis qui entre les espines
Garde ses fleurs et ses racines.
Si puis trop bien, ce m'est avis,
Comparer, se j'ay bon avis,
Au lis ma gracieuse dame   65
Dont j'aim l'onneur, le corps, et l'ame.
Vesci comment je li compere:
En ce monde n'a fors misere,
Doleurs, et tribulations,
Murmures, et temptations,   70
Tricherie, envie, mesdis,
Et barat en fait et en dis.
Ce sont les espines dou monde;
Et ma dame qu'est pure et monde
Est toudis si bien sus sa garde   75
Qu'elle entre les espines garde
Sa pais, s'onneur, sa renommée,
En fait, en dit, et en pensée.
Tant est parfaite a droit jugier
Qu'en li n'a riens a reprochier,   80
N'il n'est homs qui en puist mesdire
Pour ce qu'en li n'a que redire,
Si qu'au lis la vueil comparer,
Car je ne la puis mieus parer.

La racine qu'est enterrée   85
Puet trop bien estre comparée
A foy, car on ne la voit mie,
Et si acroist et mouteplie
Estoc, fleur, fruit, et fueille, et greinne,
Et tout a meurte ameinne.   90
Tout ensi ma dame honnourée
Est seur foy assise et fondée,
Et si fait acroistre et flourir

La grace qui ne puet mourir.
C'est l'amour de nostre signeur   95
Qui n'a pareille ne gringneur.

Encor ha le lis telle grace
Que iaue plus froide que n'est glace
Fait on de liet de sa fueille
Et de ses fleurs, mais qu'on la cueille   100
En temps, en lieu, et en saison.
Mains hommes meinne a garison
Qui sont malade de chalour—
C'est grant vertus et grant valour—
Et s'il avient qu'il ne garissent   105
Au meins leurs doleurs amenrissent.
Ne cuidiez pas que je vous ruse,
Car certeinnement qui en use
Ses maus amenrit sans delay—
Car maintes foys esprouvé l'ay.   110
Einsi garit le dous regart
De la tresbele, que dieus gart,
Les maus d'amours et assouage,
Tant est bonne, soutive, et sage.
Et se pité la fait piteuse   115
Tant que d'une larme amoreuse,
Qui maint mal garist et efface,
Arrouse les yex et la face
De son chier et loial amy,
Et qu'elle die, "Amis, aymy!   120
Pour quoy ne vous confortez vous?
Certes mes cuers est vostres tous.
Tenez, amis, je le vous baille."
Tantost sera garis sans faille,
Ne plus n'ara mestier de mire.   125
Lors dira il, "Dieus le vous mire!
Donné m'avez l'iaue de vie
De quoy ma doleur est garie,
Et s'avez mis a sanneté
Mon cuer, ma vie, et ma santé."   130

Veons que l'estoc signefie,
Qui a verge droite et polie.
Il signefie fermeté,
Vertu, force, et estableté.
Et ma dame est ferme et estable,   135
Juste, loial, et veritable.
La fueille dou lis qui est blanche,
Autant ou plus com noif sus branche,
Signefie, je n'en doubt mie,
Purté, chasté, et nette vie,   140
Sans pechie, sans tache, et sans vice,
Et sans penser mauvais malice.
Et les languettes qui y sont,
Qui greinne jaunette aus bous ont,
Signefient, qui bien s'i mire,   145
Bien penser, bien faire, et bien dire—
Bons parlers, devotes prieres,
Que nostres sires a mout chieres.
Si que de toutes ces vertus
Est li gentis corps revestus   150
De ma dame que j'aim et pris;
Et pour ce, se bien l'ay compris,
Estre doit en toute contrée
Deesse d'onneur couronnée.
Aussi le lis porte coronne   155
Si qu'en ce monde n'a personne
Qui le lis ne doie honnourer,
Amer, chierir, et aourer,
Es espines ou il demeure.
Et li vrais dieus est au desseure   160
Tous puissans, qui tant l'amera
Que des espines l'ostera,
Et li donra honneur et gloire,
Pris, puissance, pais, et victoire
Encontre tous ses anemis,   165
Si qu'einsi li lis sera mis
Hors des espines a grant joie.
Dieux doint que temprement le voie!

Et certes, quoy qui j'aie dit,
Je vueil einsi dire en mon dit   170
Que le lis est fleur masculine,
La marguerite est feminine,
Si que le lis tant s'umelie
Que suer, dame, compaigne, amie,
Royne, et maistresse l'apelle.   175
Seur toutes fleurs tant li est belle,
En li est toute s'esperance,
Son cuer, s'amour, et sa plaisence.
En li veoir tant se delite,
Tant li vault et tant li profite;   180
Car s'elle n'estoit il morroit,
Ne sans li durer ne porroit,
Dont plus se tient a honourée
Qu'avoir d'or pleinne une valée.

Or est raisons que je m'aquitte   185
De parler de la marguerite.
C'est une fleur moult gracieuse,
Mout tresbele, et mout vertueuse.
Tant a bonté, tant a valour,
Qu'an mon gré n'est plus bele flour.   190
Trop est gracieuse a mon vueil,
Et pour itant deviser vueil
Ses vertus, sa signefiance,
Et de Nature l'ordenance.
Quant Nature le devisa,   195
Certes moult longuement visa
Comment elle fust si bien faite,
Et de biauté si tresparfaite,
Qu'en elle n'eust nul deffaut
De tout ce qu'a bele fleur faut.   200
Et elle y mist si grant entente
Qu'il[11] n'est plus belle ne plus gente.
Sus .iiij. couleurs est assise,

---

[11] Ms. *Qui.*

Dont je vous diray la devise.
Nature riens n'i oublia; 205
Vert, blanc, vermeil, et jaune y a.
L'estoc est plus vert que verdure,
Qui nouvelleté nous figure;
Et quant une fleur est nouvelle,
Elle est communement [12] plus belle 210
Qu'elle n'est quant elle est marcie,
Et de sa couleur amenrie.
De fueilles a une ceinture
Si blanche qu'il n'est creature
S'il la voit qu'il ne s'en resjoie, 215
Car le blanc signefie joie.
Sus son chief ha une coronne
De quoy Nature la coronne
Com dame, maistresse, et royne
De douceur et de biauté fine. 220
La couronne est toute vermeille,
Qui trop bien au blanc s'appareille,
Si que blanc et vermeil ensamble
L'embellissent mout, ce me samble.
Mais la vermillette coulour 225
Signefie honte et paour;
Et dame qui est paoureuse,
Et de sa nature honteuse,
C'est ce qui s'onneur sauve et garde
Quant elle est simplette et couarde. 230

Une greinne a toute jaunette
Qui est si plaisant et si nette
Qu'il semble qu'elle soit dorée,
Einsi Nature l'a formée.
Mais c'est mervilleuse chose, 235
Quar quant la marguerite est close,
En ses fueilles enseveli,
Ha son tresor aveques li—

---

[12] Ms. *communenement*.

C'est sa greinne qui samble or fin.
Et croy qu'elle le fait a fin   240
Que sa greinne ne soit gastée,
Ravie, tollue, ou emblée.

Encor, mais qu'il ne vous anuit,
Vous diray qu'elle fait de nuit.
Entre ses fueilles est si close   245
Qu'il n'i puet entrer nulle chose,
Et se met en .i. moncelet—
Certes la n'a il riens de let.
Einsi par nuit elle se cuevre,
Et au matinet sa descuevre.   250
Lors la voy volentiers de l'ueil,
Car elle aoure le soleil;
Et toute jour quel part qu'il tourne
De li encliner ne sejourne.
Et samble qu'elle ait cognoissance   255
Dou soleil et de sa puissance
Qui fleurs, fruit, et tous biens meure
Par l'ordenance de Nature.

Encor y a un autre point
Qui vient a mon propos a point.   260
Chascuns scet c'une marguerite,
En France, en Ynde, et en Egypte,
C'est une pierre precieuse
Qu'est mout digne et moult vertueuse.
Et dames et signeurs s'en perent   265
Pour ce que plus cointe en apperent.
Sainte Marguerite jadis
Fu sainte et est en paradis;
Et aussi chascuns aperçoit
Que c'est li plus biaus nos qui soit;   270
Et je croy tout certeinnement
Que cils noms fu premierement
Que ne furent les autres noms,
Pour ce en est signés li renoms.

THE "DIT DE LA FLEUR DE LIS ET DE LA MARGUERITE" 23

Un grant acteur de medecine 275
Parle de li et determine,
Si com veu l'ay en son livre,
Que les mors puet faire revivre
Tant en fait on bons ongnemens.
Toutevoie s'il ment je mens, 280
Car je ne say riens de fisique,
Et je ne l'ay pas apris, si que
Je m'en doy bien par raison taire.
Mais encor vueil dire et retraire
Qu'elle est tresbonne pour routure, 285
Aussi est elle a briseure
De bras, de jame, ou d'autre membre.
Et encor, se bien m'en remembre,
A l'ueil de chascune personne
Est plaisant, gracieuse, et bonne. 290
Froide est et seche et restreintive,
En operation soutive;
Et s'est bonne a plaies nouvelles,
Si comme dient ceuls et celles,
Qui en usent et ont usé, 295
Et encore l'en plu hé [13]
Bonne est en bains quant on se baigne.
On en fait emplastres d'Espaigne
Qui moult sont bon et profitables
Et a meinte maladie ables. 300
Aussi uns Murs qui est sages
En fait potions et buvreiges
Qui, quant on en boit, doleurs maintes
En sont garies et estaintes.
De ceste fleur est .iij. manieres 305
Qui sont precieuses et chieres,
Et qu'on prise moult grant avoir;
Chascuns la desire a avoir.
Mais vraiement la plus bassette

---

[13] This line is evidently defective. It lacks a syllable and the sense is unclear.

Qu'est plus [14] pres de terre, c'est ceste 310
Qui marguerite est appellée;
Ne ce n'est pas chose celée
Qu'elle est de si grant excellence
Qu'elle honneure la science
De medecine avec l'acteur, 315
Qui n'est mensongier ne menteur;
Quar de garison s'entremet
En tous les lieus ou on la met
Tant est issue de bonne aire.
Einsi ma dame debonnaire 320
Refroide, seche, et fait garir
Tout maus amoureus et tarir;
N'en monde on ne porroit trouver
Dame qui si sceust ouvrer
En l'amoureuse maladie 325
Comme elle fait. C'est grant maistrie,
Quar y n'est lieus ou on la mette
Que d'alegier ne s'entremette
Tous ceaus qui ont mestier d'aye.
Par ma foy c'est grant signourie, 330
Mais elle le fait sagement,
Doucement, honnourablement,
De cuer, de pensée, et de fait,
Si que riens n'i ha contrefet.
C'est grant grace que dieus li donne, 335
Qui n'a nombre, terme, ne bonne,
Et si fait tout a sa loange
Et a s'onneur, einsi l'enten ge.
Or querez dame que ce face,
Qui de la douceur de sa grace 340
Puet garir tous maus amoreus,
Ja ne seront si dolereus.
Sa couleur qu'est blanche et vermeille,
Qui n'a seconde ne pareille,
Est si tresclere qu'on s'i mire 345

---

[14] Ms. *plus plus*

Clerement, qui bien la remire;
La voit on bien s'il y a tache
Qui le cuer de l'amoreus tache.
De ses dous yeus douceur douce ist
Qui l'amoureus mal adoucist,   350
Et en regardant de legier
Le fait garir et alegier.
Sa bouchette qui toudis rit
De sa douceur les amenrit,
Et son tresdous parler ensengne   355
Les amans, que chascuns se tiengne
Gais, chantans, cointes, et jolis,
Humbles, amoureus, et polis,
Et qu'il suffre les maus d'amer
Qui sont tout dous sans riens d'amer,   360
Et qu'il servent treshumblement
Leur chiere dame, et loyaument,
Quar y n'est cuers que humilité
Ne face fondre en amité;
Et sa maniere les chastoie   365
Et d'amer les met en la voie.
C'est le miroir ou il prennent
Le bien et l'onneur qu'il aprennent.
Son tresdous maintieng leur commande
Que chascuns a bien faire entende,   370
Et leur promet si riche don
Com de merci le guerredon,
S'umblement et loiaument servent
Et s'il sont tel qu'il le desservient;
Car cils qui loiaument ne sert   375
Merci ne joie ne dessert.
Einsi ma dame souvereinne
Toute doleur a santé meinne;
C'est grace de dieu par ma foy;
Milleur raison ni say ne voy.   380

Or ay ma dame comparée
A la fleur de lis, et parée

Son gentil corps de ses fueillettes
Qui sont a odorer doucettes.
De la marguerite ensement   385
Li ay je fait un vestement
Dont elle se cointoie et pere
Pour ce que plus cointe en appere.
Or vueil faire conclusion
De mon dit par condition   390
Qu'il ne vueille a nelui desplaire
Ce qu'en diray, car il doit plaire,
Pour ce que diray verité,
Raison, justice, et equité,
Tant ont loange et grace et pris,   395
Et si ay d'elles tant apris
Qu'assez loer ne les porroie,
Ne leurs bien dire ne saroie,
Tant en y a, tant en y truis;
Et mieus vorroie estre destruis   400
Que d'elles vous deisse rien
Que tout ne fust honneur et bien.
Toutevoie tant en diray
Et puis mon ouevre fineray,
Tout veu, tout consideré,   405
Vertu, grace, douceur, biauté.
Pour chose que d'elles soit ditte
Ne lairay qu'a la marguerite
Ne me teingne tant com vivray,
Car mis en ses las mon vivre ay;   410
Or vueille dieus qu'elle soit moie,
Qu'en ce monde plus ne vorroie
Que li pour avoir esperence,
Joie, pais, merci, souffissance,
Pris, et honneur, loange, et gloire   415
En la fin, et tresbon memoire.

Explicit le dit de la fleur de lis et de la Marguerite.

Analysis of the above text reveals a work of some complexity and considerable poetic merit. The thirteen divisions of the poem are of uneven length, but rhetorically they are quite logical. The first two (ll. 1-42) are introductory: The poet professes his ignorance but vows to do his best in celebrating the *fleur de lis* and the *marguerite,* and he invokes the help of God. In the next five parts (ll. 43-184) the lily is the subject. The narrator notes that Jesus Christ in his own *chansonnettes* compared the lily to his beloved: "As the lily among thorns, so is my love among the daughters" (Canticles II:2). This same statement, says the narrator, can be applied to his lady, who is perfection among the ills and sins of the world. Her faith, like the flower's unseen root, makes grace to grow which may not die. And as the lily manufactures a water which cures fever, so her tears of pity can heal the lover, who will praise that *iaue de vie.* The lily's stem is a figure for the lady's firmness, the white flower for her purity, and the little tongues of the filaments for her proper speaking and devout prayers. The poet predicts that God will take the lily from among the thorns and will give it a place of honor and glory, and victory over its enemies.

At this point the writer makes a curious statement which evidently refers directly to the lovers whose relationship evoked the work. The *lis* in his *dit,* he says, is a masculine flower and the *marguerite* is feminine (ll. 170-172). Such a remark is not simply a reference to the grammatical gender of the flowers' names; it rather capitalizes on the grammatical circumstances of the gender to give some broad hints about the real subjects of the poem. One infers that, though in the poem the virtues of both flowers are compared to those of the lady, the lily is also an apt symbol for the lover, and the Marguerite for the beloved: The two flowers, then, perhaps represent a member of the royal house of France and a lady named Marguerite. [15]

The Marguerite is celebrated in the next five sections (ll. 185-380). It is said to have four colors: a very green stem; a cincture of white petals signifying joy; a red crown which symbolizes the lady's modesty; and yellow *greinne,* the flower's treasure which it

---

[15] The poet-narrator in the dramatic scheme of the work (as distinct from the real poet, Machaut) is, of course, a surrogate of the lover. This narrator in turn uses the symbolism of the flowers to speak of himself and his beloved in the third person.

locks tightly in its petals at night. In the daytime it adores the sun, inclining to it whatever way it goes. Interrupting now rather abruptly the description of the flower, the poet digresses to talk about other uses of the word *marguerite*. It designates, he notes, a powerful and precious stone with which lords and ladies adorn themselves; *Sainte Marguerite* too has been canonized and is in Paradise; and *Marguerite* is a familiar lady's name, the most beautiful possible and the first among names.

Returning to the flower, the poet notes that a great writer of medicine has spoken of the flower in his book.[16] This writer claims that if one makes an ointment of the marguerite, it can even revive the dead. The poet cannot vouch for the truth of this, but he knows that it is good for rupture, broken bones, and all kinds of sickness, even as his lady can cure all maladies of love, however serious. A healing sweetness issues from her eyes and from her mouth when she laughs or speaks; her gentle deportment teaches each to do well and earn the mercy of his beloved.

In the concluding section (ll. 381-416), the poet recalls that he has compared his lady to the *fleur de lis,* and made her a vestment of the Marguerite with which she may dress and adorn herself. He hopes that he has praised the flowers correctly and given no one offense. Finally he proclaims that he will serve the Marguerite as long as he lives, for it can supply him with all good things.[17]

This poem, though found in only one manuscript,[18] ranks among the best of Machaut's works both in poetic interest and quality. And aside from its literary merit it is important for its

---

[16] I have not identified the "grant acteur" of l. 275, nor the "Murs qui est sages" of l. 301.

[17] This statement again indicates that the Marguerite specifically (as opposed to the lily) is to be identified with the beloved.

[18] The reason for the absence of *Lis et Marguerite* from most of the collections seems to be lateness of composition. The other manuscripts either were transcribed before it was written or were derived from such earlier manuscripts. The later Marguerite poets and Chaucer probably became acquainted with *Lis et Marguerite* from individual copies of the work, though none of these is known to survive.

place among the French poems of the Marguerite group and for its contribution to Chaucer's work. In the next chapter I take up the connections of *Lis et Marguerite* with other fourteenth-century poetry, as shown by similarities in phraseology and diction.

CHAPTER II

THE INFLUENCE OF *LIS ET MARGUERITE*

Manifold connections of *Lis et Marguerite* with other French Marguerite poems¹ are quite apparent, particularly with the central poems of the group, those which feature descriptions of the flower: Froissart's *Dittié de la flour de la Margherite*,² Deschamps' *Lai de Franchise* and Balade 539,³ and Machaut's own *Dit de la Marguerite*. One theme, for example, used by all three poets is that of the flower's devotion to the sun. At the beginning of *Dit de la Marguerite* the narrator proclaims:

> J'aim une fleur qui s'uevre et qui s'encline
> Vers le soleil, de jour quant il chemine;
> Et quant il est couchiez soubz sa courtine
>   Par nuit obscure,
> Elle se clost, ainsois que li jours fine.

In *Lis et Marguerite* (ll. 249-256), written later,⁴ he again reports the Marguerite's habit of facing the sun throughout the day and

---

¹ Professor Lowes takes up the interrelationships of the other French poems and mentions the numerous works related to the group, pp. 594-611.

² *Œuvres de Froissart: Poésies*, ed. Auguste Scheler, 3 vols. (Brussels, 1870-72), II, 209-215. Citations herein from Froissart's poems are from this edition.

³ Eustache Deschamps, *Œuvres complètes de Eustache Deschamps*, ed. le marquis de Queux de Saint-Hilaire and Gaston Raynaud, Société des anciens textes français, 11 vols. (Paris, 1878-1904), II, 203-214; III, 379-380. Citations herein from Deschamps' works are from this edition.

⁴ For several reasons I assume that composition of the *Dit de la Marguerite* antedates *Lis et Marguerite*. In the various Machaut manuscripts

closing at night, attributing the flower's behavior to its adoration of the sun and its seeming knowledge of the sun's power. Lines from Froissart's *Dittié* in turn combine the substance of both poems of Machaut:

> Car tout ensi que le soleil chemine
> De son lever jusqu'à tant qu'il decline,
> La margherite encontre lui s'encline
>   Comme celui
> Qui moustrer voelt son bien et sa doctrine;
> Car le soleil, qui en beauté l'afine,
> Naturelment li est chambre et courtine.   (ll. 53-59)

Here the Marguerite's customary following of the sun is once more discussed.[5] Froissart's *courtine* associated with the sun and the other *-ine* rhyme words seem particularly indebted to the *Dit de la Marguerite*, while the flower's display to the sun of *doctrine*

---

the works are arranged in the approximate order of composition, and *Dit de la Marguerite* precedes *Lis et Marguerite* in the one manuscript collection in which they both appear (B. N. français 22545-46). Furthermore, *Dit de la Marguerite* is a part of four collections while *Lis et Marguerite* appears in but one. Finally, the historical connnections of the two poems, which I discuss in the second part of this article, offer strong evidence of the chronological precedence of *Dit de la Marguerite*.

[5] The same general idea is developed in Deschamps' *Lai de Franchise*:

> Mais encor a trop naturel vigour,
> Car au souleil quant il rent sa luour
> S'euvre la flour, tant est humble et humaine;
> Et l'enclinent fait devers lui son tour,
> Et au vespre, quant il fait son retour,
> Ses fueilles clot que nul ne la malmaine.   (ll. 40-45)

It is also present in Chaucer's Prologue to the *Legend*:

> And whan that hit ys eve, I renne blyve,
> As sone as evere the sonne gynneth weste,
> To seen this flour, how it wil go to reste,
> For fere of nyght, so hateth she derknesse.
> Hire chere is pleynly sprad in the brightnesse
> On the sonne, for ther yt wol unclose.   (F 60-65)

The indebtedness of Chaucer and Deschamps for this imagery to both Machaut's and Froissart's works seems general rather than specific, though the ordering of Chaucer's statement and the poet's eagerness to be with the flower perhaps associates his passage more closely with *Lis et Marguerite* (ll. 249-256). References to Chaucer's works herein are from F. N. Robinson, ed., *The Works of Geoffrey Chaucer*, 2nd ed. (Boston, 1957).

seems directly connected with the daisy's imputed *cognoissance* of the sun in *Lis et Marguerite* (l. 255).

That Deschamps made use at first hand of *Lis et Marguerite* in *Lai de Franchise* is shown by his association of the lady's moral qualities with features of the flower:

> L'estoc a vert, s'a de fin or la graine;
> Blanc et vermeil lui ont donné coulour.
> Par l'estoc vert fermeté la demaine,
> Le blanc purté chascun jour lui admaine,
> Et le vermeil lui rent honte et paour;
> La graine d'or monstre sa grant valour
> Et comme elle est en tous temps pure et saine. (ll. 33-39)

These lines are a condensation of several different passages of *Lis et Marguerite*. Deschamps uses the description of the Marguerite in that poem (ll. 207, 223, 225-226) for his expression of the greenness of the stem, the *blanc et vermeil* of the petals, and the red color's symbolization of the lady's *honte et paour*. For the moralization of the stem and the white color, on the other hand, Deschamps resorted to Machaut's description of the lily, in which it is stated that the upright *estoc* signifies *fermeté* (ll. 131-133) and the white "purté, chasté et nette vie" (ll. 137-140).[6]

The list of associations of *Lis et Marguerite* with contemporary French poems may be expanded considerably, as a perusal of the texts readily indicates. The repetition of the same details in several works often makes it difficult to assign a definite line of influence, but there can be no doubt that *Lis et Marguerite* is another central member of the group. As such it evidently influenced Chaucer's Prologue to the *Legend* both directly and indirectly.

---

[6] Deschamps' Balade 539 also borrows from the same passages of Machaut's work:

> Tresdoulce fleur toute blanche et vermeille,
> A l'estoc vert et a la grayne d'or,
> Qui au monde n'avez pas vo pareille,
> Mais vous avez un singulier tresor;
>   Seurté par l'estoc vert
> En voz œuvres et en voz fais appert,
> Et par le blanc Purté en vous habite,
> Par le vermeil Paour vous suit et sert;
> Vostre nom est precieux, Marguerite. (ll. 1-9)

It shows indirect influence on the Prologue in a narrative element such as the lover's custom of watching the flower open and close. No such motif is present in *Dit de la Marguerite*. In *Lis et Marguerite* the motif appears but seems a casual circumstance:

> Einsi par nuit elle se cuevre,
> Et a matinet se descuevre.
> Lors la voy volentiers de l'ueil.   (ll. 249-251)

Froissart elaborates in the *Dittié*, transforming the willing inspections made by Machaut's lover into an obsessive habit:

> Car n'ai aultre desir
> Que de l'avoir pour veoir à loisir
> Au vespre clore et au matin ouvrir.
> Et le soleil de tout le jour sievir.   (ll. 162-165)

Chaucer in turn expands on Froissart. His narrator, with a like obsession, walks in the meadow night and day to observe the flower:

> In my bed ther daweth me no day
> That I nam up and walking in the mede
> To seen this flour ayein the sonne sprede,
> What it upryseth erly by the morwe.   (F 46-49)

> And whan that hit ys eve, I renne blyve,
> As sone as evere the sonne gynneth weste,
> To seen this flour, how it wol go to reste,
> For fere of nyght, so hateth she derknes.   (F. 60-63)

The line of influence here is quite clear, Chaucer's debt to *Lis et Marguerite* being incurred via Froissart.[7]

An element appearing in the Prologue which has an uncertain line of transmission is the description of the flower's closing at night. Such a description appears in several poems, but only in *Lis et Marguerite*, Deschamps' *Lai*, and Chaucer's Prologue is the

---

[7] Lowes (p. 613) thought that for lines 47-48 quoted above, Chaucer also used Deschamps' *Lai de Franchise* (ll. 27-30). The relationship seems tenuous, but in any event has no important bearing on the development here postulated.

flower in its closing said to be protecting itself. The dangers which it is avoiding differ: in *Lis et Marguerite* she closes to guard her golden treasure, in the *Lai* to secure herself from slander, and in the Prologue she acts simply from fear of night (F 63, 199). Nevertheless the motif of protection seems definitely to relate the passages in the three poems to each other. *Lis et Marguerite* is the earliest of the three, but whether Chaucer derived the idea at first hand from it or from the *Lai* cannot be stated with certainty.

Direct influence of *Lis et Marguerite* on Chaucer is almost certain, though no single parallel offers conclusive proof of it. Chaucer's indebtedness to the phraseology and sentiments seems likely in several passages of the Prologue, as in the resolve of the narrators to love the daisy until death. Machaut's narrator says,

> Ne lairay qu'a la marguerite
> Ne me teingne tant com vivray,
> Car mis en ses las mon vivre ay;
> Or vueille dieus qu'elle soit moie.   (ll. 408-411)

The lover in the Prologue likewise states,

> Ant I love it, and ever ylike newe,
> And evere shal, til that myn herte dye.
> Al swere I nat, of this I wol nat lye.   (F 56-58)

Machaut's narrator will not abandon the daisy as long as he lives; Chaucer's will love it ever till his heart dies. As if confirming a relationship between the passages the narrator's claim in the *Legend* that he tells the truth, though he forbears swearing, seems aimed directly against Machaut's exclamatory "vueille dieus" (l. 411).[8]

Another interesting parallel involves entirely different parts of the poems. In this case the life of the lover is represented as

---

[8] For ll. 56-57 of the Prologue Lowes (p. 615) cites Froissart's *Dittié*:

> Comme celle est que j'aim d'entente pure,
> Et amerai tous jours, quoi que j'endure.   (ll. 81-82)

"Quoi que j'endure" clearly means "Whatever I suffer," not "Until I die," so that the correspondence suggested is rather vague. Lowes adduces no parallel for Chaucer's l. 58.

dependent on the lady's presence. In *Lis et Marguerite* the lily's existence is said to be dependent on its seeing and being with the Marguerite:

> En li veoir tant se delite,
> Tant li vault et tant li profite;
> Car s'elle n'estoit il morroit.   (ll. 179-181)

Even so in the *Legend* the presence of Alceste saves the narrator:

> For, nadde comfort been of hire presence,
> I hadde ben ded.   (F 278-129)

The conditional statements ("If she were not, he would die"; "If her presence had not been, I would have died") are strikingly similar.

Other congruencies in phraseology between the works might be cited, but no one similarity is so compelling as to constitute proof of Chaucer's direct use of *Lis et Marguerite*. The same statement might be made about the line-for-line parallels which Lowes finds between the Prologue and other Marguerite poems. Lowes' study leaves no doubt of Chaucer's use of the works as a group, but as has been shown elsewhere [9] the particular uses of particular lines which he lists are often open to question. Such uncertainty regarding sources results to a large extent from the nature of Chaucer's borrowing from the French poets for the Prologue. It is not a case of word-for-word translation, as it is for many lines in the *Book of the Duchess;* what is involved is rather a selection of words and images which are frequently common to the whole group.

Such parallels as were cited above nevertheless incline one strongly to the opinion that Chaucer borrowed from *Lis et Marguerite* for the Prologue. Two other aspects of Machaut's poem offer further compelling evidence of a connection: Alceste's daisy-

---

[9] Marian Lossing, "The Prologue to the Legend of Good Women and the *Lai de Franchise,*" SP, XXXIX (1942), 15-35, shows that none of the individual correspondences which Lowes finds between Deschamps' *Lai* and the Prologue provides proof of Chaucer's use of the *Lai*.

like clothing has its only real antecedents in *Lis et Marguerite,* [10] and the opening lines of Chaucer's poem have significant similarities to Machaut's beginning.

The imagery associating the daisy with apparel is not so elaborate in *Lis et Marguerite* as in Chaucer's Prologue. Machaut depicts the Marguerite as having a girdle of white and a crown of red (ll. 213-224), a pleasant image for the white of the petals with their red tips [11] though not visualizable in anthropomorphic terms. At the end of the poem Machaut refers back to this rudimentary clothing image, stating that from the Marguerite he has made his lady a robe with which she may adorn herself (ll. 385-388). From these suggestions Chaucer seems to have developed the costume of Alceste, though he necessarily transforms Machaut's figurative equivalences so as to accomodate the features of the flower to the queen's human figure. He depicts Alceste's gown as possessing the green of the flower's foliage, while her crown is a counterpart to the whole bloom. The white *flowrouns* are carved from a single pearl, and correlatives for the yellow center and the red tips are supplied by a "fret of gold above" (F 225) and inset rubies (F 534).

The opening lines of the two poem have a less apparent but genuine similarity. In these passages both narrators muse over puzzles of existence and man's inability to explain them. Though the specific puzzles which preoccupy them differ the poets present them in like ways. Chaucer begins the Prologue with a statement of what he has heard about heaven and hell, and then comments that no one in this world has been to those places to test reports:

> Ther nis noon dwelling in his contree,
> That eyther hath in hevene or helle ybe,
> Ne may of hit noon other weyes witen,
> But as he hath herd seyd, or founde it writen;
> For by assay ther may no man it preve. (F 5-9)

---

[10] Miss Lossing (pp. 33-34) shows that the analogue to the clothing imagery found by Lowes in the *Lai de Franchise* is illusory.

[11] Our conception today of the daisy, as a flower with all-white petals, is somewhat different from that of the Marguerite poets and Chaucer, who all speak of it as being white and red with a yellow center.

Machaut begins *Lis et Marguerite* by discussing the mystery of why various flowers have different colors. I known no one, he says, who understands the secrets of nature to the point that he can tell the cause, though it is sure that many have tried with all their power (ll. 1-22). Thus to begin their works both poets broach a subject about which they state that men are ignorant, discuss the possibility of men informing themselves about it, and conclude that attempts to do so are futile. Each narrator, moreover, proclaims his personal ignorance in the same kind of adversative clause. "And as for me," says Chaucer's narrator, "though that I konne but lyte..." (F 29), while Machaut's protests, "Though such sense as nature gives me is worth very little..." (ll. 23-24).

It is not for the *Legend,* however, that Chaucer made most evident use of the opening parts of *Lis et Marguerite,* but rather for the *House of Fame.* The *House of Fame,* like Machaut's poem, begins with a section in which scientific inquiry is discussed —inquiry into the nature of dreams in Chaucer's poem, into the colors of flowers in the French work. Furthermore, in the second section of the beginnings of each work there is an invocation to God along with an expression of hope that the poem will exercise a good effect on its readers. Together with this similarity in overall plan of the beginnings is one in phraseology, first of all in the expression of puzzlement *why* one thing and *why* another:

> And why th'effect folweth of somme,
> And of somme hit shal never come;
> Why this is an avisioun
> And this a revelacioun,
> Why this a dream, why that a sweven,
> And noght to every man lyche even;
> Why this a fantome, why these oracles,
> I not.   (ll. 5-12)

> Pour quoy les unes sont blanchettes,
> L'autre est jaune, l'autre est percette,
> L'autre ynde, l'autre vermillette,
> N'i a celle qui n'ait verdour
> En esté et diverse odour,
> Ou qui n'ait ou greine ou semence,
> Ce seroit moult belle science.   (ll. 4-10)

The narrator of the *House of Fame* states, moreover, that he will not busy his brain about the *miracles* of dreams, using terms like those which Machaut uses in representing scientists who painfully inquire into the *secrets of nature:*

> But whoso of these miracles
> The causes knoweth bet then I,
> Devyne he; for I certeinly
> Ne kan hem noght, ne never thinke
> To besily my wyt to swinke,
> To knowe of hir signifiaunce
> The gendres, neyther the distaunce
> Of tymes of hem, ne the causes,
> Or why this more then that cause is.   (ll. 12-20)

> Mais je ne congnois creature
> Qui tant des secrez de nature
> Sache, qui me sceust aprendre
> Pour quoy c'est ne la cause rendre,
> Comment que c'est chose certeinne
> Que pluseurs s'en sont mis en peinne
> Et fait tout leur pooir sans feindre,
> Mais onques ne poient ateindre
> Ad ce que la chose sceue
> Fust clerement et congneue.   (ll. 11-20)

Stylistic similarities, as well as similarities in content, show up in both sets of parallel passages quoted above. In both cases loose, very involved syntax is used; as Chaucer's first fifty-two lines form one syntactical unit, so Machaut's first thirty-four lines likewise have no major break. Furthermore, both beginnings have an unusual frequency of run-on lines and polysyllabic rhymes.

One other feature of *Lis et Marguerite* possibly connects it to Chaucer's work: it is the only French Marguerite poem in which the meaning *pearl* for *Marguerite* is alluded to.[12] In Chaucer's *Legend* similarly —though the name *marguerite* is not used— the daisy and the pearl (forming the crown of Alceste) both figure.

---

[12] See ll. 261-266. Oriental lands, which Machaut associates here with the pearl (*India* and *Egypt*, l. 262), are named in different connections in other Marguerite poems: *Cyprus* and *Egypt* are named in the *Dit de la Marguerite*, p. 129, and *Egypt* is mentioned by Froissart in his *Dittié*, l. 21.

Machaut's digression on the pearl also serves to connect French Marguerite poetry somewhat more closely to two other English works, Usk's *Testament of Love* and *Pearl*, in both of which the gem is central and identified as a *margery* or *marguerite*, though the flower is not mentioned. [13]

In sum the importance of *Lis et Marguerite* is considerable. Of itself it is perhaps the most substantial of the French celebrations of the Marguerite, combining variety of subject matter with lyricism and attractive imagery. It is the last and longest of Machaut's Marguerite poems, and it seems to have had an essential role in the development of Froissart's and Deschamps' works in the group. Evidently it also had important influence on Chaucer, especially on the Prologue to the *Legend*. Finally, its status as an occasional poem supplies the scholar with valuable clues for understanding the Marguerite poems as a group and can help him to draw inferences about a great deal of other late fourteenth-century poetry. Consideration of the occasion which educed *Lis et Marguerite* is a subject for the next chapter, where I will deal with its historical filiations after first taking up Machaut's Sixth Complaint and *Dit de la Marguerite*, both of which preceded *Lis et Marguerite*.

---

[13] The signification *pearl* by forms of *Margaret* was common in English from pre-Conquest times. *OED* does not record the meaning *daisy* before the sixteenth century. See *OED*, s. v. Margaret, Margarite, Margery, Marguerite.

Chapter III

PIERRE OF CYPRUS AND THE IDENTITY OF MARGUERITE

Probably the most intriguing problem presented by French Marguerite poetry and by Chaucer's Prologue to the *Legend* concerns the identity of the lady who is celebrated. Is she an historical character or an ideal in the minds of the poets? If historical, do the three French poets deal with one or several ladies? Is she, or are they, named Marguerite, or is that simply a complimentary epithet? For the answers to such basic questions the scholar has had very little evidence. An acrostic in the first stanza of Machaut's Sixth Complaint, however, provides important factual information relevant to these questions, while at the same time identifying the work as another Marguerite poem.

The initial letters in the first stanza of the Complaint, read downward, form the acrostic:

> *M*on cuer, m'amour, ma dame souvereinne,
> *A*rbres de vie, estoile tresmonteinne,
> *R*ose de may de toute douceur pleinne,
>   *G*ente et jolie,
> *V*ous estes fleur de toute fleur mondeinne
> *E*t li conduis qui toute joie ameinne,
> *R*uissiaus de grace et la droite fonteinne;
>   *J*e n'en doubt mie.
> *T*oute biauté est en vous assevie
> *E*t vo bonté nuit et jour mouteplie;
> *P*our ce plaisence ha dedans moy norrie

> Joie sans peinne,
> Et si m'a tout en vostre signourie
> Rendu et mis, et par noble maistrie
> Ravi mon cuer qui usera sa vie
> En vo demeine. [1]

When U and I are used for their equivalents V and J, the first letters are seen to spell MARGUERITE / PIERRE. The acrostic is hardly a matter of happenstance: *Pierre* undoubtedly refers to Pierre de Lusignan, King of Cyprus, whom Machaut memorialized in his long verse-chronicle, *Prise d'Alexandrie*. This identification is corroborated by another poem of Machaut's, the *Dit de la Marguerite*, in which a lover represented as being in Cyprus or Egypt —both important sites for Pierre's operations— is associated with the flower, the Marguerite. Prosper Tarbé indeed, on the basis of the *Dit* alone, hypothesized that it was composed for Pierre, [2] and John L. Lowes substantially agreed with his hunch. "Instead of embodying a love-affair of Machaut's own," says Lowes, the *Dit de la Marguerite* "connects itself with the King of Cyprus —or at least with some friend of the poet's who, like Chaucer's Knight, attended on the brilliant fortunes of the king." [3] However, Ernest Hoepffner, the editor of Machaut's longer poems, did not agree; he thought that the poet was writing to a lady of his own:

> Pierre de Lusignan pourrait, en effet, s'exprimer ainsi; mais il nous semble que ce n'est là qu'un lieu commun de la poésie amoureuse, et l'on aurait tort d'attribuer à ces mots un sens plus précis et une signification littérale, et de voir, par conséquent, dans ce poème la preuve de relations personnelles entre le roi de Chypre et le chanoine de Reims. [4]

---

[1] *Poésies lyriques*, ed. V.-F. Chichmaref (Paris, 1909), I, 256. Subsequent references herein to the Complaint are to this edition.

[2] Prosper Tarbé, *Œuvres de Guillaume de Machaut* (Paris, 1849), pp. xxviii-xxix. References herein to the *Dit de la Marguerite* are to Tarbé's edition, pp. 123-129.

[3] John L. Lowes, "The Prologue to the *Legend of Good Women* as Related to the French Marguerite Poems and the *Filostrato*," PMLA, XIX (1904), 595-596.

[4] Ernest Hoepffner, *Œuvres de Guillaume de Machaut* (Paris, 1908-1921), I, xlii-xliii. Hoepffner supports his denial of the *Dit's* relationship to

The acrostic in the Sixth Complaint enables us now to state confidently that Machaut wrote both the Complaint and the *Dit de la Marguerite* for Pierre, and that he no doubt was personally acquainted with the King. While Machaut's third Marguerite poem, the *Dit de la fleur de lis et de la Marguerite*, has no apparent connection with Pierre, certain hypotheses about its historical filiations may be based on a consideration of the other two works. The career of Pierre, then, provides a starting point for analyzing the historical circumstances of all three.

The facts of Pierre's career and the manner in which the contents of the Complaint and the *Dit de la Marguerite* fit into his biography indicate that his lady Marguerite was historical, a real individual; at the same time, other facts regarding Pierre's use of the name *Marguerite* lead to the surmise that the name denoted to the king —and by extension the poets— certain ideal qualities which transcend the individual woman. The daisy in the Prologue to Chaucer's *Legend* seems likewise to embody such symbolism.

Pierre is a fascinating figure. Born in 1329, member of a western dynasty which established itself in the East in the late twelfth century, in name King of Jerusalem as well as monarch in fact of trade-rich Cyprus, he as a child had a vision in which God summoned him to the "saint passage," a new crusade.[5] When he assumed the throne in 1359, his desire to recover for himself and Christendom all of his nominal domain was nourished by his own ambition and enterprise, by the zeal of Pierre de Thomas —Patriarch of Constantinople and later papal legate for the Crusade [6]—

Pierre by noting that in Machaut's *Lis et Marguerite* there is nothing "qui vise tout particulièrement le roi de Chypre," a circumstance which is discussed below.

[5] *La Prise d'Alexandrie ou chronique du roy Pierre Ier*, ed. Louis de Mas Latrie (Geneva, 1877), ll. 299-332. See Aziz S. Atiya, *The Crusade in the Later Middle Ages* (London, 1938), pp. 319-321, for a brief account of Pierre's young life.

[6] For accounts of this courageous and wholly dedicated churchman, who has failed of canonization though he is recognized as a saint by the Carmelites and in the Bollandists' *Acta Sanctorum*, see Frederick J. Boehlke, Jr., *Pierre de Thomas: Scholar, Diplomat, and Crusader* (Philadelphia, 1966); and two eulogistic contemporary biographies: *The Life of Saint Peter Thomas by Philippe de Mézières*, ed. Joachim Smet, O. Carm. (Rome, 1954), also

and by his chancellor, Philippe de Mézières, who throughout most of his long life had a singleminded dedication to the reconquest of the Holy Land.[7] In October 1362 Pierre with his two counsellors set sail for Europe to enlist support for a new crusade. They proceeded from Venice through the major cities of northern Italy to Avignon, where on Good Friday 1363 King Pierre and Jean II of France, enthusiastically supported by Urban V, took up the Cross.[8] Pierre then embarked on a tour through the rest of Western Christendom seeking help.

England was one of his first stops. There he was entertained in the sumptuous manner in which a proud court might be expected to fete an imposing eastern monarch who was undertaking the ultimate task of the Christian knight. Though he gained from Edward III only token support for his Crusade,[9] in England as everywhere he made a great impression on those who observed him, including two literary personages, Chaucer and Froissart.[10] Chaucer subsequently associated his Knight with Pierre's greatest successes, *Alisaundre*, *Satalye*, and *Lyeys;* and his Monk tells the story of Pierre's murder, in which the king's "chivalrie" is especially emphasized. Froissart in both chronicle and verse evidences great admiration for this king, "tant creus et honneurés et de raison,"[11] and in the *Joli Buisson de Jonece* he states explicitly that Pierre became his patron and benefactor.[12]

---

published by the Bollandists for January 29; and the life by Jean de Carmesson, part of which is edited by Louis de Mas Latrie, *Histoire de l'Ile de Chipre* (Paris, 1852-61), II, 281-284.

[7] For Philippe's life, see especially Neculai Jorga, *Philippe de Mézières (1327-1405) et la croisade au xive siècle* (Paris, 1896); also Atiya, Chap. VII, pp. 128-154.

[8] Froissart has the fullest account of Pierre's and Jean's assumption of the Cross; *Chroniques de J. Froissart*, ed. Siméon Luce et al. (Paris, 1869-1957), VI, 82-85. See also *Prise d'Alexandrie*, ll. 661-730; and Smet's edition of Philippe's *Life of Saint Peter Thomas*, pp. 105-106.

[9] *Chroniques,* ed. Luce, VI, 89-92.

[10] Froissart was Queen Philippa's secretary from 1361 to her death in 1369.

[11] *Chroniques,* ed. Luce, VI, 84.

[12] Et c'est raisons que je renomme
De Cippre le noble roy pere,
Et que de ses bienfais me pere.

Œuvres de Froissart: Poésies, II, ll. 348-350.

After Pierre had recrossed the Channel and visited the Black Prince at Angoulême, his plans suffered a stunning setback with the death in February 1364 of King Jean, the Crusade's leader. Pierre in May was in Reims for the coronation of Jean's son, Charles V, for which occasion Machaut, Canon of Reims, perhaps composed the Mass. The Cypriot monarch accompanied Charles back to Paris for the great celebrations there, and he lost no opportunity to enlist support for his project from the new king and his *baronnie*, who were all in attendance.[13] Although many promised help, the most important, Charles, excused himself because of problems at home. But even as his failure with the king in London was now repeated in Paris, Pierre once more made a great impression on a man of letters, Guillaume de Machaut, who was to be his celebrant in the *Prise d'Alexandrie*. Machaut does not describe his initial meeting with Pierre; however, it is evident that his abiding interest in the man began at the time of the Coronation, for it is precisely from this date that he tells Pierre's story in detail.[14]

From France Pierre went through Germany preaching the Crusade at various courts; he had an historic conference at Cracow with Emperor Charles I and the kings of Hungary and Poland; thence he proceeded to Austria and finally Venice, where he was reunited with Pierre de Thomas and Philippe de Mézières, who had likewise been exerting continual efforts in behalf of the Crusade. From there, accompanied by a modest assemblage of ships and fighting men (which included none of the important rulers whose help Pierre had solicited[15]), they set sail for the East.

Spectacular success was theirs in October 1365 when they took Alexandria; but they did not capitalize on this success. Over the protests of King Pierre and Pierre de Thomas,[16] the bulk of the crusaders chose to abandon the city rather than face the imminent counterattack of the heathens. After pillaging and burning, they took their booty and sailed home. Of necessity Pierre sailed

---

[13] *Chroniques*, ed. Luce, VI, 98-99, 108-109, 132-134; *Prise*, ll. 731-838.
[14] As Machaut's narrative of Pierre's activities becomes much more detailed, Pierre recedes from Froissart's history.
[15] *Prise*, ll. 1895-1914; Smet, pp. 120-121.
[16] *Prise*, ll. 3386-3539; Smet, pp. 133-134.

with them. His life subsequently was marked by minor successes and major disappointments. Adversity mounted and triumphed. Pierre de Thomas, the iron-willed soldier of the Church, died in Cyprus in 1366; the Venetians, displeased that trade had been seriously damaged by the raid on Alexandria, courted the pagan potentates; and Europe was increasingly embroiled in internal differences. Rather than support for his efforts to mount still another Crusade, Pierre found opposition on all sides, even from the Pope. Confined in his operations, he became abusive to the Cypriot nobility, and a group of them surprised and killed him one night in 1369 while he was with a mistress.[17] He was only forty.

Machaut's report of Pierre's death, which reflects the same historical tradition as the Monk's tragedy,[18] differs from the apparent facts. The *Prise d'Alexandrie* has it that he was killed in bed by envious followers, mentioning nothing about the mistress who was with him. In other respects Machaut's history, as Mas Latrie states, seems quite accurate;[19] indeed, despite his obvious bias in Pierre's favor, the poet relates quite straighforwardly most of the unpleasant events of the king's last few months which are mentioned by the other chroniclers. But the praise for Pierre with which *Prise d'Alexandrie* closes is unqualified, as is the condemnation of the assassins. Machaut would make his hero the tenth Worthy:

> Il fu si vaillans, c'est la somme,
> Que ce sera honneur et preuz
> S'il est mis avec les ix. preus;
> Si que ce sera le disiemes,
> Car einsi comme nous disiemes
> Quant nous avons parlé de li,

---

[17] For the events preceding and attendant on the assassination, see especially Leontios Makhairas, *Recital concerning the Sweet Land of Cyprus entitled 'Chronicle'*, ed. and trans. R. M. Dawkins (Oxford, 1932), I, 214-269; also both chroniclers in *Choniques d'Amadi et de Strambaldi*, ed. René de Mas Latrie (Paris, 1891-93), I, 419-426; II, 92-114.

[18] *Prise*, ll. 7956-8827; Monk's Tale, B 3581-88. On the sources of Chaucer's version see Haldeen Braddy, "The Two Petros in the 'Monkes Tale,'" *PMLA*, L (1935), 69-80.

[19] Mas Latrie discusses the historical accuracy of Machaut's chronicle in his introduction to the *Prise*, pp. xviii-xxii.

Onques riens ne li abeli
Tant comme honneur, chascuns le voit.   (ll. 8851-58)

The exalted opinion which Machaut had conceived of Pierre upon meeting him in 1364 was never lowered. He remained in the poet's mind the vigorous young king who dazzled all onlookers, especially when he was in full armor:

> Et quant il estoit bien armez,
> Bien montez et bien acesmés,
> Le lance eu pong, l'escut au col,
> Il n'i avoit sage ne fol
> Que ne deïst à grant murmure:
> "Cils roys fu nez en l'armeüre;"
> Tant estoit gens, joins, lons et drois,
> Hardis, puissans en tous endrois.   (ll. 855-862)

In retrospect Machaut still marvelled at the sight:

> Et je meïsmes m'en merveil,
> Quant à li pense et je m'esveil.   (ll. 874-875)

All of Europe, to be sure, admired him. Urban V customarily referred to Pierre as his "athlete of Christ." [20] The adulation of Pierre by his devout and idealistic chancellor, Philippe de Mézières, was undiminished till his death in 1405. [21] Froissart and Petrarch himself, normally hostile to the Cypriot French, felt that Pierre's murder inflicted a severe loss on Christianity. [22] Even the modern historian, who might find good reason to impugn Pierre's motives and character, is attracted to him. Aziz Atiya in his standard history of the later crusades states of Pierre:

---

[20] Jorga, *Philippe de Mézières*, p. 341. Jorga notes (p. 340) that Urban also saluted Pierre as "athlète intrépide et lion valeureux."

[21] A remark by Philippe in his *Life of Saint Peter Thomas* (p. 104) exemplifies his idolization of the man whom he served as chancellor. He speaks of Pierre de Thomas's enterprises as legate for the Crusade: "Et sicut Paulus nomen Christi coram regibus et principibus portabat, ita legatus nomen regis coram papa, cardinalibus et principibus magnificabat et passagium annuntiabat." The comparison, then, is Pierre de Thomas to Paul and King Pierre to Christ.

[22] *Histoire de l'Ile de Chypre*, II, 337.

The King's will to take the Cross was actuated mainly by his desire to serve God and his resolution to deliver the Holy Land from the oppressive hand of the infidels. His birth, his education, the state of his kingdom, the traditions of his house, the bent of his mind, and the influence of his close friends and supporters — all these factors collaborated to make to Pierre an ideal crusader; and the genuineness of his feeling for the cause was less unmixed than in the case of any contemporary monarch. He was the real 'athleta Christi'. [23]

Such is the man who is the lover-narrator of Machaut's Sixth Complaint and the *Dit de la Marguerite*, both poems no doubt written in the years after the coronation of Charles V in 1364, when the poet must have first met Pierre. The situations represented in the two poems coordinate with biographical information about Pierre to suggest certain things concernings his activities, the lady's identity, and the occasion of the poems. Summaries of the works will help to bring these out.

The 208-line *Dit de la Marguerite*, like *Lis et Marguerite*, influenced later poems by Froissart and Deschamps, and evidently Chaucer's Prologue to the *Legend*. Divided into thirteen stanzas of sixteen lines each, it is ostensibly about the flower known as the *marguerite*, but this flower clearly symbolizes a woman. The flower has great powers, says the narrator at the beginning, for from across the sea (p. 124) it has cured him of his sickness. From the time he first saw it he became its servant, and though he now sees it "po sovent" (litotes for "not at all," one assumes), he remains devoted; for Souvenirs and Doulz Pensers recall the flower to him, and when the wind blows from its "dous pays" he grows healthier (p. 126). Thinking of it he knows that one who is fortified with the flower need not fear pain, death, or peril.

If such joy comes from remembrance, he continues, how much greater will it be when he sees the flower. Yet if he cannot do that, he will still serve it loyally "en tous lieus" (p. 127). Even from "d'outre la mer" (p. 127) it seems to be present to him, and everything he has comes from it. When he is in Cyprus or Egypt, he states in concluding, his heart remains with the *Marguerite*:

---

[23] P. 323.

Et quant je suis en Chipre ou en Egypte,
Mes cuers en li tres doucement habite.   (p. 129)

Since the poem represents the narrator as "over the sea," stock terminology for the Eastern Mediterranean area, the time in question would seem to be after Pierre sailed from Venice in 1365. Furthermore, mention of Egypt indicates a time after the attack on Alexandria, since the destination of the Crusaders was not determined till after the fleet assembled at Rhodes, and points of attack other than Egypt would have been equally logical for them.[24] Pierre, then, is probably back in Cyprus after the battle, while the flower (and the lady the flower stands for) is somewhere on the mainland.

The Sixth Complaint, of which the first stanza (containing the acrostic) has been quoted, seems on the other hand to have been composed while Pierre was still in France. Its 192 lines are made up of twelve stanzas of the same form as the *Dit de la Marguerite*, but the flower allegory is not used, the poem being explicitly addressed to a lady. In fact, though the lady is identified as *Marguerite* acrostically and is called "rose of May" and "flower of all flowers," the Marguerite flower is not specifically mentioned. After according the lady effusive praise in the initial stanza, the narrator alludes to his impending departure and discusses his relationship with her. He knows, he says, that he can never merit her least reward, yet he will serve her always faithfully. Unable to conceive that she will not have pity on him who will never have comfort without her, he hopes to see her before he leaves; but if he doesn't he will carry Bon Espoir, Souvenir, and Dous Penser with him (ll. 73-75). Far away from her he will be armed and protected by these, and he will take comfort in her great nobility, goodness, beauty, and sweetness.

The main problems he foresees are that he will lack the sight of her, Dous Regart, which has fed him with its "amoreuse

---

[24] Atiya notes (p. 347), "It was rumoured in the ranks that the armies of the Cross were to be disembarked somewhere on the coast of Asia Minor or Syria. Even many of the leaders of the host who moved in the higher circles remained in the dark." Since Pierre's major successes before Alexandria had been in Asia Minor, Machaut would likewise have had no reason to connect Pierre with Egypt because of previous exploits.

pasture" (l. 118), and that Tristece will attack him so that he will be unable to survive. At this point he seems to suggest that she can do something to relieve this problem:

> Si qu'en vous est de moy faire ou deffaire,
> Mais riens nulle qui vous peüst desplaire
> Ne me porroit. (ll. 142-144)

But if he is suggesting that she come with him to supply Dous Regart, he does not follow up the suggestion; rather he continues on the assumption that they will be separated and states that if he does anything which merits honor it will be because of her. He concludes by congratulating himself for loving her and by expressing the hope that she, who has neither "pareille ne seconde" (l. 182), will one day call him Ami. She is so pure, he concludes,

> Qu'en Ynde n'a si precieuse jasme,
> De vo douceur vaurroit mieus une drasme
> Que tout le miel et le sucre et le basme
> Qui est en monde. (ll. 189-192)

Chronologically, it seems that the Complaint precedes the *Dit de la Marguerite*. In the Complaint the narrator anticipates the solace which Souvenirs and Dous Pensers will provide when he is separated from his lady, and in the *Dit* these two actually comfort him in his separation; in the former he is about to part from her, and in the latter he writes from overseas. If one assumes then that the Complaint was written while Pierre was still with Machaut in France, it dates from late spring 1364; if the *Dit* was composed after the news of Alexandria's capture reached Europe, it was written in 1366 or later. [25]

Though in both works the narrator speaks of the lady in hyperbolic terms which seem extravagant even in medieval love

---

[25] Lowes estimates (pp. 595-596) that "The *Dit* was written somewhere between 1364 and 1369 —not improbably during the former year." In setting 1364 as a *terminus a quo* he either ignores the implications of the dramatic situation in the poem (the lover is overseas), or else he does not apply this situation literally. The contents of the *Complainte* and the *Dit*, of course, provide a valuable contrast not available to Lowes for determining the situations envisioned in both poems.

poetry, he apparently refers to a real lady, one whose presence he enjoyed for a time and from whom he was later separated. That she was in the ordinary sense one of Pierre's mistresses, as Lowes infers, is doubtful, for it is improbable that the King paid much attention to politically inconsequential ladies while touring Europe with the red cross of the Crusader on his coat and the whole Near East on his mind;[26] and it is even more improbable that at this time he valued any lady's charms so much for their own sake as to have a canon of Reims write a poem to celebrate them. Pierre's activities at the coronation especially were concentrated on convincing Charles, his supporters, and anyone who might exert influence on them to associate themselves with his Crusade.

On Machaut's part, surely his admiration of Pierre resulted rather from the king's dedication to the primary goal of the Christian knight, the recovery of the Holy Land, than from his amatory prowess. Machaut was a love poet by avocation but a cleric by profession; devotion to the cause of Christianity rather than polite pandering would seem to explain his role. The works in their historical context, therefore, have most point as courtly compliments to a grand lady who might help Pierre gain support for his projects.

Conjecture about the identity of the particular lady is made difficult by the popularity of the name, and is further complicated by the fact that the lady's name may not have been Marguerite. The French word *marguerite* bears the signification and potentially the symbolic value of an admired flower and a precious gem; one may refer to his beloved as a *pearl* or a *daisy* without her name being Pearl or Daisy. However, it is more probable than not that the vogue of Marguerite poetry was stimulated initially by a lady who was baptized *Marguerite*.

Previous critics have speculated with diffidence about her historical identity. Tarbé says that the name was made fashionable in the fourteenth century by the wife of Saint Louis, Marguerite

---

[26] Froissart states explicitly (*Chroniques,* ed. Luce, VI, 84) that Jean and Pierre followed the established custom of literally bearing a cross (probably sewn) on their garments: "Tout ensi que vous poés oïr, emprisent et enchargièrent, dessus leur deseurain vestement, la vermelle crois, li rois Jehans de France et li dessus nommet [i. e., Pierre]."

of Provence. He notes that Saint Louis, Philippe III, Philippe IV, and Philippe V each gave the name to a daughter, and that Louis X married Marguerite of Burgundy. In the light of such currency Tarbé declines to conjecture about the lady's specific identity:

> Nous pourrions multiplier les citations, mais ce serait sans résultat utile; nous n'avons pas trouvé quelle princesse fut aimée de Pierre de Lusignan. [27]

Lowes points to this note of Tarbé and to the several columns of Marguerites listed in the index of DuCange's *Les Familles d'Outre-Mer*, [28] and he similarly concludes, "Which one of the numerous Marguerites of the day the poem celebrates, one must leave undertermined." [29] Both critics were looking in unlikely places. The women cited by Tarbé were in their prime long before Pierre's heyday; and, if the testimony of the poems is to be trusted, the lady concerned did not belong to a French family of the East —the subject of DuCange's study— but rather resided in Europe.

One imagines that in addition to her being a resident of Western Europe she was personally known to both Pierre and Machaut, that French was her native language, and that she was in a position of particular power whereby she might assist the Crusade at the time of Pierre's tour of Western Europe. This set of requisites is filled particularly well by Marguerite of Flanders, daughter of Louis de Mâle and widow of Philippe de Rouvre, Duke of Burgundy, who from the date of her widowhood at age eleven in 1361 till her remarriage in 1369 to the second Philippe of Burgundy was "unquestionably the most important heiress of the day." [30]

The acquaintanceship of both Pierre and Machaut with this lady may be assumed. She and they undoubtedly attended the

---

[27] Pp. 185-186.
[28] E.-G. Rey, ed., *Les Familles d'Outre-Mer de DuCange* (Paris, 1869), pp. 951-953. The index indicates that Marguerite was the most popular female name among these families, even more than Marie.
[29] P. 596.
[30] Sidney Armitage-Smith, *John of Gaunt* (New York, 1964), p. 29.

coronation at Reims and the celebrations in Paris which followed.[31] Pierre also would have been with her when he was entertained at Louis' court at Ghent.[32] Machaut's familiarity with her family is evidenced to us by Deschamps, who delivered a copy of the older poet's *Voir Dit* to Louis, and reports its reception in a *balade*.[33] Machaut's lengthy autobiographical romance was better calculated to please the women of the family, one would think, than the practical Louis.

The young widow's prospective inheritance comprised "fiefs of France and of the Empire, the wealth of Flanders, and lands stretching into the very heart of France."[34] She was courted assiduously by both the King of France and the King of England, the former proferring his brother, the latter his son. Edward III had apparently won out in October 1364 when Louis de Mâle agreed to the marriage of his daughter with Edmund, Duke of Cambridge. However, when the necessary dispensation for consanguinity was refused by the Pope, the way was cleared for eventual French victory. Yet Marguerite's marriage to the brother of Charles V, Philippe le Hardi, was not effected till June 19, 1369.

Marriage negotiations were particularly intense while Pierre was touring Europe.[35] Certainly he would have found it expedient to play up to this young lady whose inheritance was so coveted by both England and France.[36] At the same time he no doubt

---

[31] The attendance of Pierre and Marguerite's mother and grandmother at the coronation is a matter of record. *Chroniques des règnes de Jean II et de Charles V*, ed. R. Delachenal (Paris, 1910-20), II, 2-3.

[32] The exact time of Pierre's visit to the Flemish court, whether before or after his visit to England, is disputed. In any event it is agreed that Louis de Mâle treated him with special honor. See Jorga, pp. 173-174, 190.

[33] In this poem Deschamps tells Machaut that the "Monseigneur de Flandre" received graciously "Vostre Voir Dit," and had him read from it with many knights present; *Œuvres complètes de Eustache Deschamps*, I, 248-249.

[34] Armitage-Smith, p. 29.

[35] Edward III opened negotiations in 1362, but it was only after the coronation, when Pierre had gone on to Germany, that Louis de Mâle came to an agreement with the King of England. See *Chroniques*, ed. Luce, VI, 77, 174-175; VII, 129-131. See also Armitage-Smith, pp. 28-32; and especially F. Quicke, *Les Pay-Bas à la veille de la période bourguignonne* (Brussels, 1947), pp. 75-78, 139-145.

[36] As is no doubt the case with many ladies who were subjects for medieval love poems, Marguerite's personal appearance and character would

curried the favor of both her mother and grandmother (Louis' mother), two other Marguerites of power at the Flemish court.[37] Machaut may very well have assisted Pierre's attentions to these ladies with his poetry, first with the Complaint containing the acrostic (a trick to please the young especially) and then with the *Dit de la Marguerite*. Pierre would have had no ambitions to marry Marguerite, of course; being married and occupied with a crusade, he needed allies, not a wife —especially not one whom his major prospective allies coveted.

If these speculations have validity, Pierre is perhaps in Paris and she in Ghent when he expresses in the Complaint (or rather Machaut expresses for him) determination to see her before he leaves if at all possible:

> Mais se je puis trouver voie ne tour,
> Par quoy puisse veoir vo cointe atour,
> Einsois que parte ou face mon retour,
>   Je le feray.
> Et se j'y fail, en peinne et en labour,
> Dolens de cuer, en tristece et en plour,
> Pleins et espris d'amoureuse dolour
>   Me partiray.   (ll. 65-72)

Whether he saw her again before setting out for Germany and Eastern Europe is problematical. It was probably two or three years later that Machaut had occasion to write a second poem to

---

not have entirely satisfied the encomiums of Machaut's verse. Though in 1364 she probably possessed the attractiveness of youth, according to Ernest Petit she was not beautiful. Petit further states that it was only despite egotistical and domineering temperaments that she and Philippe le Hardi had a successful marriage. See Petit, *Ducs de Bourgogne de la maison de Valois*, I (Paris, 1909), 10-11. Because of Marguerite's powerful position Philippe probably made way for her from the beginning. Froissart says that she "estoit bien dame, car le duc son mary ne l'euist point voulentiers corrouchie, et bien y avoit cause, car de par la dame le duc tenoit grant foison de beaulx et bons et grans héritages, et si en avoit de beaulx enffans, de quoy le duc estoit plus tenu à elle." *Œuvres de Froissart*, ed. Kervyn de Lettenhove (Brussels, 1867-1877), XIV, 351. The "grans héritages" could doubtless move a poet as well as tame a duke.

[37] Marguerite of Brabant, the wife of Louis de Mâle, was the second daughter of Jean III of Brabant. Louis' mother, Marguerite of France, was the daughter of Philippe V of France.

Marguerite for Pierre, who was still working for a crusade and needed powerfull allies more than ever. In the *Dit de la Marguerite* the narrator is depicted as separated by the sea from his beloved; he can only imagine his happiness if he ever sees the lady again:

> Et quant par li si grant joie me vient
> Toutes les fois que de li me souvient,
> Cent mille fois doublera, s'il avient
>   Que je la voye.   (p. 126)

But Pierre's fortunes never brought him back to France. He was assassinated in January, 1369. That same spring Louis de Mâle agreed to the marriage of Marguerite with Philippe le Hardi, Duke of Burgundy, and the wedding took place in Ghent June 19.

The third Marguerite poem of Machaut, the *Dit de la fleur de lis et de la Marguerite,* seems to involve a suitor other than the King of Cyprus. In this work the poet states that the lily is "fleur masculine" and the marguerite "feminine" (ll. 171-172).[38] Since the *fleur de lis* is not part of the Lusignan coat of arms, the reference apparently is not to Pierre; rather the symbol strongly suggests the royal family of France. The ceremony at Ghent allied the *fleur de lis* of the king's brother with the Marguerite.

That Machaut should have written this poem to Marguerite on the part of the French royal family, even were he personally unacquainted with Philippe, is not improbable. He had known the lady and her family for at least several years, and had previously sponsored Pierre's polite attentions to her. At the same time, the successful sealing of this alliance was a matter of great national interest for any Frenchman. Over and above these factors is the poet's friendship of more than fifty years with Philippe's family. Some of Guillaume's most important poetry celebrates various of the Duke's closest relatives.

Machaut's young adulthood had been spent in the service of Philippe's grandfather, Jean of Luxembourg; from 1323 to 1346 Machaut was his clerk and secretary.[39] Jean is the title figure of the poet's *Jugement dou Roy de Behaingne* and the subject of

---
[38] See discussion above, p. 25.
[39] For Machaut's life, see Hoepffner, I, xi-xliii.

a eulogy in his *Prise d'Alexandrie* (ll. 771-798). Jean's daughter Bonne, the wife of Jean II of France and mother of Philippe, is also celebrated in the *Prise:* the poet calls her *ma dame* and the best lady in the world; I ought to know, he says, for I served her greatly (ll. 763-770). In the same poem he also speaks admiringly of all four of Bonne's sons, including Philippe the warrior:

> Charles, Loeys, Jehan, Phelippe,
> Qui moult en armes se delite.   (ll. 797-798)

He goes on to praise Charles V especially (ll. 799-804); in *Voir Dit,* furthermore, he clearly implies that he was one of the trusted intimates of Charles.[40] Another brother of Philippe, the Duke of Berry, is the subject of Machaut's long *Dit de la Fonteinne amoreuse;* in that work the poet depicts himself as companion and comforter of the young duke. Machaut thus proclaims a close association with Philippe's grandfather, his mother, and two of his brothers; he had no doubt known Philippe himself from infancy.

If one considers the familiarity of the poet with the royal family and Philippe's well-known liberality in the patronage of the arts, Machaut's composition of *Lis et Marguerite* as a personal service to Philippe seems almost indicated. There is certainly no other romantic occasion of Machaut's later years, involving a couple fitly symbolized by a *fleur de lis* and a *marguerite,* for which the work might more probably have been written.

The text of the poem suggests that it was composed at the time of the final marriage negotiations in 1369. In the *Chroniques* Froissart tells how Louis de Mâle eventually obtained *quittances* from the agreement with Edward III since the Pope continued obdurate against Marguerite's marriage with Edmund. With the encouragement of his mother, Marguerite of France,[41] Louis

---

[40] Hoepffner, I, xxxvii.

[41] For the role of Marguerite of France in the marriage negotiations, see H. Pirenne, *Histoire de Belgique,* II (Brussels, 1922), 191. Her behavior at this time became legendary; see *Biographie nationale de Belgique,* XIII, col. 633. Historical records also testify to the strength of her character; see L. Stouff, "Marguerite de France, comtesse de Flandre, d'Artois et de Bourgogne et sa ville d'Arbois," *Annales de Bourgogne,* III (1931), 7-37.

entered into serious negotiations with Charles, which soon resulted in a marriage which pleased all France:

> Tantost apriès ceste ordenance, on proceda ou mariage qui se fist et confrema en le bonne ville de Gand. Et là eut grans festes et grans solennités, au jour des noces, devant et apriès, et grant fuison de signeurs, barons et chevaliers. [42]

Thus the heiress was delivered from the clutches of the English. The narrator of *Lis et Marguerite,* who devotes the first part of the work to a discussion of the *lis,* makes a great deal of the biblical poet's comparison of his beloved to a lily among the thorns. Even so may his lady be compared, says the narrator. The thorns are identified as the evils of the world in general —"Doleurs, et tribulations, / Murmures et temptations" (ll. 69-70)— but it takes no great stretch of the imagination to equate the thorns with the English who had virtually surrounded Marguerite for several years.

Indicating that final delivery of the lily from the thorns had not been accomplished at the time of composition of *Lis et Marguerite,* the narrator expresses confidence that the true God so loves her that he will take her from among the thorns and give her honor and glory, and victory over her enemies: "May God grant it soon!" (ll. 160-168). The later short discourse on the name Marguerite also seems to have particular topical relevance. The narrator states that Marguerite is the most beautiful name there is, that this name moreover preceded all other names (ll. 271-274). This apparently excessive praise, which puts Queen Jeanne of France, the Blessed Virgin, and Eve in second place, is explained by the fact that Marguerite is the name not only of the influential heiress but also of her mother and of her powerful grandmother, the daughter of Philippe V. By 1369 the line of impressive Marguerites seems to stretch back almost to pre-history.

The rest of the work does not seem to have special topicality. In the final lines, however, one imagines that the narrator has

---

[42] *Chroniques,* ed. Luce, VII, 130.

the current marriage negotiations in mind when he prays to God that his beloved will be his:

> Or vueille dieus qu'elle soit moie,
> Qu'en ce monde plus ne vorroie
> Que li pour avoir esperence,
> Joie, pais, merci, soufissance,
> Pris, et honneur, loange, et gloire
> En la fin, et tresbon memoire.   (ll. 411-416)

The appropriateness on all scores of *Lis et Marguerite* to the alliance of Phillippe le Hardi and Marguerite of Flanders tends to substantiate the hypothesis that she is the Marguerite of Machaut's two earlier poems. It also suggests that the same lady may have been a subject for the later works of Froissart and Deschamps.

Of the numerous works of those two poets which belong in one way or another to Marguerite poetry, the *Lai de Franchise* is the most definitely placed in time and space: May 1385 at the Chateau of Beauté-sur-Marne.[43] Lowes was confident that Deschamps had written the poem for the daughter of Marguerite of Flanders, Marguerite of Burgundy (the fourth in line of the name), to commemorate the celebration following her marriage in April 1385 to Guillaume of Hainault. This was a double wedding in which a second child of Marguerite of Flanders, the future Jean sans Peur, married the sister of Guillaume of Hainault, who was also Marguerite. In drawing his conclusion, Lowes summarizes:

> During the preceding two months [February and March 1385], Marguerite de Bourgogne had been, with her mother, a frequent visitor at the Chateau de Beauté, and it would be most natural that in a poem written during the festivities which followed her marriage and preceded her departure, a courtly compliment should be paid her by the poet. And as a matter of fact it is, as the closing lines declare, specifically to the flower that the *Lay* is dedicated, and that, too, *au departir*.[44]

---

[43] See Lowes, pp. 603-607; and Raynaud in *Œuvres de Deschamps*, XI, 45-46.
[44] Lowes, 606-607.

In the light of the close family associations, whether the flower addressed represented Marguerite of Burgundy, or a composite of the two brides, or Marguerite of Flanders, is a matter of secondary consequence in the establishment of the historical relevance of the *Lai* to Machaut's poems. It would be quite natural for a poet who had in mind the earlier works to associate the symbolic flower with the daughter (or daughters) of the same name as well as with the original Marguerite. Yet in the light of Deschamps' close relationship over a long period with Marguerite of Flanders one suspects that she, rather than her daughter, is the flower to whom the *Lai* is addressed.

Deschamps had known her at least from the time years earlier that he had delivered a copy of Machaut's *Voir Dit* to the court at Ghent. The poet came to count both her husband and her son among his primary benefactors, mentioning them several times in his works.[45] In other of his poems he mentions Marguerite of Flanders too, addressing her on occasion in a quite familiar manner, twice as *Belle-Tante,* and in a *balade* by the Flemish diminutive of Marguerite, *Guillequine.*[46]

Gaston Raynaud believes that other of Deschamps' Marguerite poems are addressed to a nun, Marguerite la Clinete,[47] and to Marie of Hungary, "qu'il s'obstine avec Froissart à nommer *Marguerite.*"[48] Raynaud seems to lack substantiating evidence for these identifications, particularly for the latter. At the same time, a theory that all of Deschamps' Marguerite poems were written for Marguerite of Flanders would not be reasonable; and it is significant in considering the poetic conception of Marguerite that other ladies —even ladies with different baptismal names— are possible subjects.

Among Marguerite poems Froissart's seem the least localized, the least designed for a particular occasion, and hence the least assignable to particular ladies.[49] Whether the daisies he celebrates

---

[45] Raynaud lists the references of the poet to these two Dukes of Burgundy, *Œuvres de Deschamps,* XI, 263.
[46] *Œuvres de Deschamps,* XI, 262.
[47] XI, 271.
[48] XI, 47.
[49] Lowes discusses Froissart's Marguerite poetry pp. 597-603. Neither Raynaud (quoted above), who thinks that Froissart referred to Marie of

and the Marguerites he alludes to refer to Marie of Hungary, Queen Philippa of England, or a series of ladies, the clues seem too sparse to say definitely. His close association with Wensceslas of Brabant makes it certain that he would have been familiar with Marguerite of Flanders, who was closely related to Wenceslas and his family by blood, geographical considerations, and political interests.[50] As with Deschamps, however, it would be difficult to imagine that Marguerite of Flanders was the lady concerned in all of Froissart's Marguerite poems. The *Paradys d'Amours*, for instance, which contains the famous *balade*, "Sus toutes fleurs j'aime la margherite," was written before 1369, no doubt while Froissart was still in England.[51]

The fact that the works of Froissart and Deschamps probably cannot all be tied to one particular lady simply points to a feature that seems characteristic of Marguerite poetry from it inception, which is that the name Marguerite and the flower denoted by the name embody a transcendent ideal of which any single woman is only a temporal embodiment. This symbolism probably originated with Pierre of Cyprus, and will be discussed in the concluding chapter.

Hungary, nor other critics have cited substantial evidence in the poetry which would point to one lady rather than another. Recently Margaret Galway in "The 'Amie' of Froissart," *N&Q*, IV (1967), 330-332, has put forward Marie de Châtillon, Duchess of Anjou.

[50] Wenceslas was maternal uncle of Philippe le Hardi; Wenceslas' wife Jeanne was maternal aunt of Marguerite of Flanders. The courts of Brussels and Ghent were less than forty miles apart. According to Froissart, it was Duchess Jeanne of Brabant who almost singlehandedly brought about the double wedding (discussed above) between the children of Philippe and Marguerite and those of House of Hainault. His account suggests that social relations between the courts of Brabant and Burgundy were very close. See *Chroniques*, ed. Luce, XI, 186-195.

[51] In the *Book of the Duchess*, composed in 1369, Chaucer made use of the *Paradys*.

Chapter IV

THE TRANSCENDENT MARGUERITE

Circumstances in the background of Pierre of Cyprus, and facts about him reported in the chronicles, support the notion that Marguerite to him was more than the name of a particular lady. In the first place the original Saint Marguerite came from very close to his home. Though there were several later medieval Saints Marguerite, the third-century lady of Antioch was *the* saint of that name to all the Middle Ages, as the life in the *Golden Legend,* for example, testifies.[1] Her eastern origin perhaps accounts largely for the particular vogue of the name among French families in the East.[2] Secondly, Pierre's country was particularly rich in pearls *(marguerites)* if one is to believe a chronicler such as Makhairas, who reports the great prosperity of the island in Pierre's time. One of the merchants was so rich, he states, that when he had the king to dinner he burned aloes logs instead of wood, and that "instead of sweetmeats" he gave away pearls to his guests from a great dish which it took four men to carry.[3] Pierre himself evidently had a liking for regal dress adorned with pearls. An Arabic chronicler reporting the capture of Alexandria tells how a Jew sent by the governor of the city to negotiate with Pierre found the King in a tent overlooking the sea. "He was dressed in precious

---
[1] Ed. H. Graesse, 3rd ed. (Bratislava, 1890), pp. 399-403.
[2] See Chapter III, footnote 28.
[3] Dawkins, I, 81-83.

robes embroidered with gold and *studded with pearls*, and he wore a gold crown surmounted by a *glittering pearl*." [4]

Perhaps it was a result of the local origin of Saint Marguerite along with her special faith in the Cross, [5] and of the particular association of pearls with the contemporary wealth and splendor of Cyprus that the name Marguerite came to be especially meaningful to Pierre. When in the late 1360's he had a tower built —a pleasure-house by Machaut's account, but with a sinister purpose according to other chroniclers— [6] he named it the *Marguerite*. Though it is conceivable, as Lowes and Tarbé conjectured, that the name referred to the lady celebrated in Machaut's poems, [7] the fact that Pierre had two local mistresses at the time he was building the tower, and that he evidently both loved and respected his jealous Queen Eleanor, [8] would make such celebration of a foreign lady somewhat unlikely. Other associations of the name with the king revealed in the chronicle of Makhairas make the idea of an exclusive connection of it with another woman appear more improbable. Makhairas reports that the Queen, when she was attempting to evade the Genoese a

---

[4] Quoted by Atiya, p. 369. Italics mine.

[5] Saint Marguerite, who is generally depicted standing on the head of a dragon and often holding a cross, defeated the monster through the Sign of the Cross. An excellent representation of the courtly Marguerite holding a cross is found on the right-hand panel of Hugo Van der Goes' Portinari Altarpiece.

[6] Machaut, *Prise*, ll. 8360-65, 8574-79. The references to the chroniclers are contained in Lowes' long note on the tower of the Marguerite, pp. 596-597.

[7] Tarbé, p. xxix; Lowes, p. 596n. In discussing a fifteenth-century event involving the tower, Mas Latrie (*Histoire*, III, 265n) says that it was named for the Hill of Sainte-Marguerite on which it was built. He does not document this intriguing assertion, which well may reflect a confused tradition.

[8] Makhairas attests to Pierre's love for the Queen despite his attentions to two mistresses. He says that the king loved Eleanor so much that "Wherever he was, he would take her shift to lay it in his arms when he slept, and he made his chamberlain always bring with him the queen's shift, and had them put it in his bed. And if any one say, 'Seeing that he had such great love for her, how was it that he had two mistresses?' This he did on account of his great sensuality, because he was a young man." Dawkins, I, 223. Eleanor's jealousy is evidenced in the horrendous story of her cruelty to one of Pierre's mistresses told by the chroniclers. See Dawkins, I, 215-219; and Amadi and Strambaldi in *Chroniques d'Amadi et de Strambaldi*, I, 419-420; II, 92-94.

short time after Pierre's death, made good her escape on a "wonderful mule" named *Margarita* which had belonged to her husband.[9] The second daughter of Pierre and Eleanor, moreover, was christened *Margarita.*[10]

It would seem that by possessing this name the European lady, the tower, the mule, and the daughter symbolized for Pierre ideals which he associated in the first place with the appellation. Some validation of this suggestion is found in an angry outburst of Pierre to his counsellors when he was considering an accusation of infidelity against Queen Eleanor: "But I ask your advice, what do you think I should do: Shall I leave my wife and send her back to her father? Shall I kill the lousy dog who has destroyed the *pearl*,[11] or shall I not show that I have seen anything?"[12] Here the enigmatic Marguerite may be thought to embody Pierre's ideal of womanhood or queenship.[13]

The nature of Pierre's Marguerite, who is the subject of Machaut's poems, has implications for the whole group of related French works by Froissart and Deschamps, and also for the associated English works of Chaucer, Thomas Usk, and the poet of the *Pearl*. It is probable that Froissart and Deschamps, and the English writers at second hand, were privy to the personal and symbolic implications of Machaut's works. They may well have followed Machaut in making their poetic daisies, pearls, and Maid Margarets embodiments of ideals at the same time that they were specific ladies. The consistently elevated terms of description used by the Frenchmen accord with such a supposition.

---

[9] Dawkins, I, 445.

[10] Though the birth date of Margarita is a matter of interest as a signal of the development of Pierre's fascination with the name, it is not recorded in the genealogies. Since she did not finally marry till 1385, one would suspect that she was born after Pierre's return from his three-year absence in 1365. See DuCange's *Familles d'Outre-Mer*, pp. 81-82; and "Généalogie des rois de Chypre de la famille de Lusignan," *Archivio Veneto*, XI, 333-335.

[11] The Greek chronicler's *margaritarin* translates, one would assume, Pierre's French word *marguerite*.

[12] Dawkins, I, 233.

[13] It would not be reasonable, taking into account the texts of the poems, to imagine that Eleanor was herself the Marguerite of Machaut's poems.

As with the French poets, the daisy in Chaucer's Prologue to the *Legend* is described with elegant hyperbole. It is

> of alle floures flour,
> Fulfilled of al vertu and honour,
> And evere ilyke faire and fressh of hewe. [14]

But Chaucer is more specific than his predecessors about what the daisy represents. The nineteen saints of love who follow Alceste state expressly that it symbolizes the worth of them all. Kneeling before the flower they sing,

> "Heel and honour
> To trouthe of womanhede, and to this flour
> That bereth our alder pris in figurynge!" (F 296-298)

Alceste, the narrator's "lady free" (F 271), with her green clothes and her white petalled crown is a feminine embodiment of the daisy and its symbolism. Her beauty transcends the power of nature. She is

> So womanly, so benigne, and so meke,
> That in this world, thogh that men wolde seke,
> Half hire beaute shulde men nat fynde
> In creature that formed ys by kynde. (F 243-246)

Alceste is a substantial realization of the transcendent Lady Marguerite implicit in the other Marguerite poems. Machaut perhaps stimulated Chaucer's imagination by imputing anthropomorphic characteristics to the daisy in *Lis et Marguerite* when he speaks of the flower's girdle and its crown (ll. 213-224) and talks about having clothed his lady in the garb of the flower (ll. 385-388). Chaucer then exploits the ultimate possibilities of Machaut's nascent transformation of the daisy into a woman by creating the figure of Alceste, whose dress and crown give her the appearance of a daisy. At the same time Chaucer left in his poem wholly flowerlike daisies, natural symbols of womanly virtue, of which

---

[14] F 53-55. For the complex indebtedness of Chaucer's Prologue to his French contemporaries, and his acknowledgement of his borrowing (F 68-83), see Lowes, pp. 611-634, and Chapter II above.

Alceste is a supernatural embodiment. Of course Alceste may also represent a real lady —perhaps Joan of Kent— [15] just as the ideals symbolized in the French poems have human counterparts.

The Marguerite poems thus provide an example of the very fluid use of symbolism which was possible in medieval literature. In these works the flower, the pearl, the lady and the goddess are valid, interchangeable symbols for the same thing; for Pierre of Cyprus a handsome tower and a wonderful mule apparently functioned as equally legitimate embodiments of his ideal. If the symbol is chameleon, so also is the thing symbolized; to say that the flower stands for ideal womanhood is no doubt an over-simplification. While the figurative possibilities of ideal womanhood probably epitomize what the flower and other symbols stand for, at the same time they may possess the diversity of significance that Thomas Usk's "margarite-perle" has in the *Testament of Love*. "Margarite," he explains, "a woman, betokeneth grace, lerning, or wisdom of god, or els holy church." [16] Such a list, while probably not completely applicable to the works of the other poets, suggests a possible range.

This study of Machaut's three Marguerite poems has perhaps provided some insight into their appeal for the aristocratic French audiences and for Chaucer. The three may be seen as a coherent series of works which were associated with important and glamorous historical figures, and were themselves a part of history in a way that few love poems have been. The warrior-knight Pierre of Cyprus finds (conveniently) in the powerful Marguerite of Flanders an embodiment of his mystical ideal; Machaut, a poet of kings, devoted like his age to a new crusade, attempts to promote Pierre's influence with Marguerite by two poems which he composed perhaps two years apart. Later, with Pierre dead,

---

[15] Margaret Galway's theory that Alceste represents the Black Prince's widow, Joan of Kent, seems the most compelling of the several theories of this order about Alceste. "Chaucer's Sovereign Lady: a Study of the Prologue to the Legend and Related Poems," *MLR*, XXXIII (1938), 145-199.

[16] Walter W. Skeat, ed., *Complete Works of Geoffrey Chaucer*, VII (Oxford, 1897), 145. For a discussion of the symbolism in this prose work which is also relevant to the Marguerite poems, see S. K. Heninger, Jr., "The Marguerite-Pearl Allegory in Thomas Usk's *Testament of Love*," *Speculum*, XXXII (1957), 92-98.

Machaut writes *Lis et Marguerite* to support the final marriage negotiations of Charles and Philippe Valois with Louis de Mâle. The symbolism of the Marguerite, being applicable to an ideal rather than limited to a particular occasion and a particular person, lent itself to adaptation by other poets, notably Froissart and Deschamps, who adhere quite closely to Machaut's patterns. Subsequently in the Prologue to the *Legend* Chaucer develops and expands the possibilities of Marguerite poetry; despite the undoubted superiority of his poem over those of his French predecessors, the imagery and overall conception of the Prologue directly depends on and grows out of their works. Usk's long prose imitation of Boethius and the Middle English *Pearl* are not so clearly dependent on the Marguerite poems, but the symbolism of their Margery-pearls seems consonant with that of Chaucer's daisy and the Marguerites of the French writers. Thus, just as Machaut's longer narratives provided basic inspiration for the love stories of his French and English successors,[17] so his works in this lyric mode had important seminal influence on a substantial group of their poems.

---

[17] For the influence of Machaut's longer poems on Froissart and Chaucer, see my study, *Chaucer and the French Love Poets,* University of North Carolina Studies in Comparative Literature (Chapel Hill, 1968).

INDEX

Alexandria, capture of, 44-45, 48, 49
Atiya, Aziz S., 42n, 46-47, 48n, 61n
Bible, *Canticle of Canticles*, 27
Bonne of Luxembourg, 55
Charles I, Emperor, 44
Charles V, King of France, 44, 47, 52, 55, 65
Chaucer, Geoffrey, 29, 43; *Book of the Duchess*, 35, 59n; *Canterbury Tales*, General Prologue, 41, 43; Monk's Tale, 43; *House of Fame*, 10, 37-38; *Legend of Good Women*, Prologue, 9, 10, 13, 14, 31n, 32, 33, 34-37, 38, 42, 47, 62, 63-64, 65
Chichmaref, V.-F., 13, 14n, 41n

Daisy. See *Marguerite*, flower
Dante, 9
Deschamps, Eustache, 9, 13, 39, 52, 59, 62, 65; Balade 539, 30, 32n; *Lai de Franchise*, 30, 31n, 32, 33, 34, 35n, 57-58
DuCange, *Familles d'Outre-Mer*, 51

Edward, the Black Prince, 44
Edward III, King of England, 43, 52, 55
Eleanor, Queen of Cyprus, 61-62

Froissart, Jean, 9, 13, 39, 43, 46, 57, 58-59, 62, 65; *Chroniques*, 43, 44n, 50n, 52n, 53n, 55, 56, 59n; *Dittié de la flour de la Margherite*, 10, 30, 31, 33; *Joli Buisson de Jonece*, 43; *Paradys d'Amours*, 59

Galway, Margaret, 64n
Golden Legend, 60
Guillaume of Hainault, 57

Heninger, S. K., Jr., 64n
Hoepffner, Ernest, 13, 14-15, 41, 54n, 55n

Jean, Duke of Berry, 55
Jean II, King of France, 43, 44, 55
Jean of Luxembourg, 54
Jean sans Peur, 57
Jeanne, Duchess of Brabant, 59n
Joan of Kent, 64

Lossing, Marian, 35n
Louis de Mâle, 51, 52, 54, 55, 65
Lowes, John L., 14, 30n, 33n, 34n, 41, 49n, 50, 57, 58n, 61

Machaut, Guillaume de, contribution to Marguerite poetry, 10, 13, 64; association with Pierre of Cyprus, 44, 50; acquaintance with Marguerite of Flanders, 51-52; connection with Philippe le Hardi, 54-55; *Dit de la Fonteinne amoureuse*, 55; *Dit de la Marguerite*, edited by Tarbé, 14; associations with other poems, 30, 31, 33; dating, 30n, 49; connected with Pierre of Cyprus, 41-42; analysis, 47-48; situation portrayed, 54; mentioned, 13, 39; *Dit de la fleur de lis et de la Marguerite*, previously unedited, 13-14; manuscript, 14-15; edition, 15-26; analysis, 26-29; dating, 28n, 30n; influence, 30-39, 63; occasion, 42, 54-57, 65; mentioned, 10; *Dit de la Harpe*, 14; *Dit de la Rose*, 14; *Jugement dou Roy de Behaingne*, 54; *Prise d'Alexandrie*, 41, 42n, 44, 45-46, 55; Sixth Complaint, acrostic in,

10, 13, 40-42; associated with Pierre of Cyprus, 47; analysis, 48-49; mentioned, 39; *Voir Dit*, 52, 55, 58
Makhairas, Leontios, 45n, 60, 61-62
Margarita, daughter of Pierre of Cyprus, 62
Margarita, mule of Pierre of Cyprus, 62
Marguerite, historical identity in poetry, 9, 40-42, 47-59; significance, 9, 28; imagery, 10; flower, 27-28, 32-37 *passim*, 45; prominence as proper name, 28, 51n; symbolism, 50, 62, 64
Marguerite, tower of Pierre of Cyprus, 61
Marguerite, Saint, of Antioch, 28, 60, 61
Marguerite of Burgundy, 51, 57-58
Marguerite of Brabant, 53n
Marguerite la Clinete, 58
Marguerite of Flanders, in Machaut's poetry, 11, 15, 53-57, 64-65; powerful heiress, 51-52; personal appearance and character, 52n; marriage negotiations, 52-53, 55-56; in Deschamps' poetry, 57-58; Froissart's acquaintance with, 59
Marguerite of France, 53n, 55
Marguerite of Hainault, 57
Marguerite of Provence, 50-51
Marie of Hungary, 58-59
Mas Latrie, Louis de, 42n, 43n, 45, 61n

Pearl, 9, 39, 62, 65
Pearls, in Marguerite poetry, 9, 38-39; associated with Pierre of Cyprus, 60-61
Petrarch, Francis, 9, 46
Philippa, Queen of England, 43n, 59
Philippe V, King of France, 53n, 56
Philippe le Hardi, Duke of Burgundy, 15, 51, 52, 54-56, 57, 59n, 65
Philippe de Mézières, 43, 44, 46
Philippe de Rouvre, Duke of Burgundy, 51
Pierre de Lusignan, King of Cyprus, in Machaut's poetry, 10-11, 41-42, 46-50; leader of Crusade, 42-45; adulation of, 45-47; relationship with Marguerite of F l a n d e r s , 50-54; significance of *Marguerite* for, 59, 60-62, 64; relationship with Queen Eleanor, 61
Pierre de Thomas, 42, 44, 45, 46n

Raynaud, Gaston, 30n, 57n, 58

Tarbé, Prosper, 14, 41, 50-51, 61
Tyrwhitt, Thomas, 14

Urban V, 43, 45, 46, 52
Usk, Thomas, *Testament of Love*, 9, 39, 62, 64, 65

Wenceslas, Duke of Brabant, 59

Young, Karl, 14

www.ingramcontent.com/pod-product-compliance
Lightning Source LLC
Chambersburg PA
CBHW020422230426
43663CB00007BA/1280